365 DAYS OF THANKFULNESS

Emily A Knight

A simple guide to developing the
"gratitude attitude" all year long.

365 Days of Thankfulness

Introduction

Please view these writings as a guide to developing a grateful heart. Although some of the entries are personal while others are more general, all are being shared with the goal of directing our thoughts to something for which we can be thankful. I mention my parents and teachers because that is / was my experience. It is my sincere desire that we should all become more grateful for having spent a little time thinking about the many people and events the Lord has used to bring us to the place in which we find ourselves today.

Some special days remain constant with their numbers because they are dates (July 4) while others change because they are celebrated on certain days (Thanksgiving). Because of this I have included a sub-heading if the entry correlates with a holiday or yearly event. You will probably be able to tell which days were Sundays in the year these were written because those have a little more "churchy" theme. I appreciate your taking the time to read my thoughts and allowing me to share with you the people and things for which I am thankful.

Thank you for allowing me to share,

Emily A Knight

Educator / Author

Day 1 Patriotism

I am truly grateful to have been born an American citizen. Do I think everything pertaining to our country and our government is perfect? No. I do believe we have the greatest heritage for the development of any nation recorded in history. I do believe we enjoy more freedoms than any other nation on the planet today. These freedoms are being slowly encroached upon and eroded away; but, as of this writing, are for the most part still in place.

As I am preparing to move to the foreign field of Mexico I am even more grateful for America. Let us be thankful for our country. Let us be willing to stand vigilant against those who would deny our freedoms and willing to fight enemies whether within or without who would take them from us.

Day 2

I am truly grateful to have been born a Southerner and for the rich heritage that implies. Both sides of my family are rich with history, stories, hospitality, grace, and friendliness. My mom was the best cook! She could take the simplest of ingredients and make quite the feast. She always cooked things that were good for us and that my Dad enjoyed. On our birthdays she would make our favorites. To this day I have never tasted any sweet tea or sweet potato pie that could even be in the same league as my Aunt Inez's. When I was growing up *everyone* went to church, *everyone* had a job, and *everyone* was quick to help anyone in need. Even though I grew up in the city, I was raised with small-town, country values.

(Please do not read this in the wrong spirit. If you are from the North, or even a different country, please take time today to be thankful for **your** heritage.)

Day 3

I am thankful that my Mom stayed at home with my brother and me while we were little. I am thankful that my Dad worked more than one job for several years so that she could be able to do so. Even up through my high-school years, my Mom was at home. There was just something about knowing that every day I came home from school my Mom would be there. Usually, dinner was already cooking which made the house smell delicious! The house, the yard, and our clothes were always clean. Mom always wanted to hear about our day with all the details. I talked to my Mom about everything, always.

Day 4

I am thankful to have grown up in a time when people knew and helped their neighbors. Our neighborhood was very close-knit. All the kids played together with the same "rules." We were expected to obey each other's parents. We could ride our bikes for blocks without being afraid. We had the same curfew. The adults played volleyball almost every summer evening until dark, and then sat around on the patio talking. In the winter, they would play cards until it was late. Yes, I am thankful for my neighbors and my neighborhood.

Day 5

I am thankful for my parents' friends of a lifetime who encouraged me and prayed for me as a young person. These friends of my parents helped me to develop my view of the world and to find my place in it. They helped to make the world that I knew a safe, happy, and secure place. Some of these friends were from church and some were the neighbors previously mentioned. They were always there for us like family should be. During my Mom's battle with cancer our family especially felt and needed their presence.

Day 6

I am thankful for my Christian School education. I realize that my parents made many sacrifices for that to happen. I realize that my teachers also made many sacrifices for that to happen. We did not have the equipment, labs, or even a gymnasium that a public education might offer, but the principles and the philosophies gained far outweigh those negatives.

Again, please do not mis-read what I am truly saying. If you are able to read this book, you were given some type of education. Let us be grateful to those who sacrificed so that we might better ourselves.

Day 7

I am thankful that my parents taught me good habits which have developed into good character. I am thankful they forced me to brush my teeth, make my bed, go to church, and many other things. I am thankful they insisted I do my best in school regardless of the grades I received. I am thankful my Mom made me take the LifeSavers back to Kroger and apologize to the manager for stealing them, then make me ask my Dad to spank me for it so I wouldn't grow up to be a thief.

Day 8

I am grateful for my little brother.

Please spend time remembering growing up with your siblings. If they are still alive, it wouldn't hurt to call or write them to express how grateful you are that they put up with you for so many years.

Day 9

I am grateful for my aunts and uncles and cousins and the good relationship we enjoyed growing up. Every Saturday before I became a teenager was spent with my cousins. We played kickball, dodgeball, our own version of bat-ball, and every other kind of ball. If we couldn't go outside then Monopoly or Life it was. We argued, fussed, drank Kool-Aid and made up. We watched cartoons and played Barbies. (The guys played GI Joe). Every over-night adventure provided obligatory ghost stories. I am thankful for my cousins.

Day 10

I am thankful that my Mom taught me to read. As I work with children who genuinely struggle in this area, I am even more grateful that I have always enjoyed reading. Mom made it fun for me. We had little games with the words in the storybooks. I am thankful that my Mom read to us every night at bedtime. Also, as an incentive to read the Bible, lights out was lifted if we were in bed reading the Bible. Kids will do anything to keep from going to bed; why not let it be something good?

Day 11

I am grateful to have been born to parents who were raised in church. They each had a period of time in their young adult lives when they were not regularly attending church, but they knew when they had children they would want them in Sunday School and church. I truly had a rich heritage. I am grateful for being taught the importance of reverencing God.

Day 12

I am grateful for the two years I spent in Public School with teachers who taught Bible stories and kept a paddle in the classroom. My parents' mantra: "If you get a spanking at school you are getting two spankings when you get home." Too many parents have forsaken the rod. I know that sadly there are teachers now who abuse their power and sometimes even their students. Wouldn't it be better to not leave your child with someone you didn't trust? My parents met our teachers and assured them of their support regarding our expected behavior.

Day 13

I am thankful for Tom and Joyce Davis who invited my parents to the inaugural Sunday of Faith Baptist Temple in Louisville, KY. Joyce was my Mom's hairdresser and invited all of her clients to Church.

Day 14

I am grateful for the Bus Ministry and for my first Bus Captain Tom Davis who brought me to church when my parents didn't and who let me ride "just for fun" when my parents did come. Bro. Tom and Mrs. Joyce were very influential in my family's spiritual growth.

Day 15

I am thankful for my third and fourth grade teacher, Mrs. Betty Hundley. It was the first year of our new Christian school and Mrs. Hundley helped us to make a smooth and relatively easy transition from a much larger public school.

Day 16

I am thankful for all of my elementary school teachers who instilled a love for learning into my life. My sixth grade teacher, Mrs. Bailiff, especially cultivated a love for reading. She read us *The Chronicles of Narnia* every day after lunch. This collection is still among my favorite books.

Day 17

I am thankful for the friends I met in elementary school. We experienced the world together. We learned about life and love, and what makes true happiness and what doesn't. We had so much fun together it made me decide to spend the rest of my life in school. We grew up together. I am burdened for today's kids who are sheltered from life's consequences, yet not truly protected from the evils of this world.

Day 18

I am grateful for my Junior Girls' Sunday School teacher, Mrs. Lila Coffee. She sent post cards of encouragement. She visited me. She saw me as an individual. Mrs. Coffee planted seeds in my heart that took root and flourished during my teen and young adult years. Although Mrs. Coffee has gone to heaven now, I encourage you to take some time today and remember an influential Sunday School teacher in your life. Send a text or note of encouragement this week. I remember that she appreciated it so much when I would seek her out when I was home from college for Christmas or summer break.

Day 19

I am thankful for my closest friend since third grade, Debbie Myers. We *literally* grew up together. We laughed together, played together, and got in trouble together. We learned typing together way back before there were computers. We kept in touch from separate colleges when "snail mail" was our only option. Other friends have come and gone, a few have stayed the test of time, but none other for so long. How about you? Who is that friend of yours who knows everything about you and is still in your corner?

Day 20

I am forever grateful for my Junior / Senior High School English teacher, Mrs. Marianne Brown. She taught us to speak properly and to not use the fact that we were from Kentucky as an excuse to not speak properly. Of equal importance, she taught us to think and speak for ourselves and to take a stand for what we believed. She taught me that giving my all to God could never really be a sacrifice. Mrs. Brown is the reason I became a teacher. Anyone I have been used to influence owes a debt of gratitude to her as well.

Day 21

I am grateful for my Junior High history teacher, Mrs. Judy Overstreet. She helped us to understand the importance of history and our place in it. She taught us that we should never be ashamed of where God gave us our start. Wherever life has taken me, I have always been glad to say that I am from Louisville, Kentucky.

Day 22

I am truly grateful for the correction I received from my Jr/Sr High School Christian School teachers. I have previously mentioned a few of them for their particular influence, but with maturity, I can say I am also grateful for their correction. Mrs. Overstreet once assigned me twenty-five sentences because "my attitude was showing." When I handed them in with some smart-alec comment, she doubled the assignment. Another remark, the assignment was re-doubled. Before it was over, I had written the sentences *five-hundred* times! Needless to say, my attitude in history class was much improved.

Too many times we are anxious to treat our young people like the adults that they are not yet. Too many times we "overlook" snide comments or thinly veiled disrespect. This does not help the young person or their friends or siblings who see them "get away with it."

Day 23

I am thankful that my parents *always* backed my other authorities. When I "whined" about those five-hundred sentences my parents reminded me that they had also been talking to and working with me regarding my attitude. They told me that they had been praying that someone else that I loved and respected would point it out to me so that I could see the importance of correcting it. I am thankful that my parents did not have a meeting with the teacher to complain that she was too hard on me or that I had enough homework already. My mom actually made me number the sentences to make sure that I did not "accidentally" skip any. Only after I became a teacher myself did I realize what a tremendous gift I had been given by parents who always sided with my authorities.

Day 24

I am thankful that I learned the importance of soul-winning as a young teenager. Every Saturday our youth pastor and his wife took the teenagers out on different bus routes of our church. They taught us the verses to use, how to respect others and their property, and how to be a witness for our Saviour. I am thankful that this was taught to us as a way to be obedient. I have never thought about whether it was something I enjoyed or wondered whether it was "working." I believe it is what God wants me to do and so I do it. Let's go Soulwinning!

Day 25

I am thankful for a series of Sunday School lessons "Dare to be Different" that was taught to me as a young person. I had a Sunday School teacher who challenged us to be a witness and a testimony to our lost friends. The lessons were on the life of Daniel and how, as a leader, he was even more separated to God than the other Jewish boys who had been taken into captivity. Yes, we should tell people about the God that we serve; but His very presence in our lives should be so evident that they already know something is different about us. Those lessons laid the groundwork and developed attitudes in my heart that still allow me to change and grow as the Lord daily reveals His will to me.

Too many churches today have stopped teaching II Corinthians 6:17 altogether, let alone an entire series on being set apart from the world. The result is leaving us with incomplete leaders assuming the leadership roles of the next generation.

Day 26

"I LOVE Monday mornings!" ~ for six years every Monday there was school, this is the first statement our class heard. Yes, even the Mondays after Christmas and Spring Break. For this I am truly grateful. I asked Mrs. Brown about that one day – if she really did LOVE Monday mornings or if she were using reverse psychology on us. She replied that she loved Monday mornings for the same reasons that she loved September, and New Year's Day, and birthdays, and maybe even more because even if the others were all added together there would be more Mondays on the calendar than those days. Of course, I asked what you may be thinking right now: "What could those special days possibly have in common with a dreary, ordinary old Monday?" A new beginning! A fresh start! An opportunity to remind ourselves what is truly important in life. For a teacher, that is my students. I get to see all of your faces and be reminded of my reason to be here. For those who work regular jobs it is a chance to be able to provide for their families. So you see, every Monday is a new beginning!

I LOVE MONDAY MORNINGS!

Day 27

I am thankful for my high school Bible teacher, Bro. Dennis Graham. I am thankful that he read passages from the Bible then had us tell him what they meant to us. He taught us to practically apply biblical principles. He taught us not to wait until we were in college, or adults, or married, or parents, or anything else to make decisions for God. He taught us that the decision to live the Christian life was a daily decision. Every morning that you wake up decide to follow Jesus today. Tomorrow when you wake up, do the same thing. That is the secret to living a successful Christian life: it must be lived one day at a time.

"The Bible is to be lived and not just learned."

Day 28

I am thankful for sports. As a young person, I had a LOT of energy. Organized sports was a tremendous channel for that energy. I played softball, volleyball, and basketball from seventh – twelfth grades. Sports was a great way to develop friendships, learn about fairness (and sometimes un-fairness), develop teamwork, and to grow in school spirit. I am grateful for the volunteer coaches. I am thankful that my parents, even though they struggled with the school bill at times, found a way for my brother and myself to enjoy playing on the sports teams.

Day 29

I am grateful for lessons I learned from my Mom while she was going through cancer in the 1980's. Shortly after her fortieth birthday my Mom was diagnosed with ovarian cancer that spread throughout her internal organs. I hated (and still hate) cancer and what it does to a person's body. But it was powerless against my Mom's spirit.

I learned that nothing was more important to her in this life than her family: my Dad, my brother, and myself. I watched her throw up every other weekend from Friday until Sunday because of the chemotherapy. I watched her undergo more than one surgery in attempts to chop off the ugly head of cancer. I am sure there were other painful and horrendous moments that I did not see. But my Mom never stopped being my Mom. When she could, she still came to our ball games and programs. When she couldn't, she made sure that we knew she wanted to. She still oversaw our homework and quizzed us for our tests; just from her bed instead of the kitchen table. My mom told us that she was enduring all of this because she wanted to be there for us until we were raised. God had given her a job to do, and whatever it took, she was not going to let cancer keep her from doing it. Yes, I HATE cancer! But I learned so much from and about my Mom while she was going through it.

Day 30

I am thankful for the lessons I learned from my Dad while my Mom was going through cancer in the 1980's. What stands out the most right now are the things that he said and did that I thought at the time was what everyone said or did whose spouse had cancer. He went to all of the appointments with my Mom, listened to all the options, and told her that whatever she decided to do, he would stand by her and go through it with her. He did not demand that she do whatever he thought she should; it was her body and her decision. Remember with me that many of the treatments were experimental back then. He sat with her while she told us (my brother and I were teenagers) what the treatments were, when hers would start, and what she would need from us. I mentioned watching her throw up every other weekend with the chemotherapy. Every time, Dad was sitting there with her holding her hand and the bucket. My Dad talked to my brother and I about what was happening to Mom and what we should expect. Of course, many things happened for which we could not prepare. My Dad was (and is) a rock. I learned about loyalty and faithfulness. I learned about love and life.

Day 31

I am thankful that our family got to visit Disneyworld! We had so much fun! We got there as the park was opening and stayed until the fireworks parade! I remember my Dad carrying me on his shoulders so I could watch for Donald Duck. I remember riding "It's a Small World." I remember that my Mom loved the Madhatters's Teacups.

I think it is important for kids to have a good time with their family. It doesn't have to be Disneyworld. It's an opportunity for parents to show their kids they enjoy spending time with them. I don't have any idea how much that trip cost; but I know that it was worth it.

February

Day 32

I am grateful that I had the privilege of attending college. I had a period of time to learn and grow into the adult world while still enjoying the "safety-net" of home. I have friends now who were thrust into the adult world while they were really still teenagers. Whether right out of high school, or in a few cases, even before they were able to finish, their road in life was much harder and longer than mine. Some missed out on the opportunity because of their own doing. Some missed the opportunity because of illness; their own or a family member's. Some missed this opportunity because of finances. I am truly grateful that I was provided the opportunity to better myself in an institute of higher learning.

Day 33

I am thankful for the privilege of attending a Christian college. I made friends for a lifetime. I learned invaluable life truths. I was able to spend my formative young adult years with those who reinforced the values that my parents, my youth pastor, and my teachers had instilled in me. I was able to participate in a chapel service which daily challenged me to become a leader of my generation. I am thankful that I was able to study at a Christian college.

Day 34

I am thankful for my first college roommate and friend still today, Suzanne Lester White who encouraged me, prayed with me, and accepted me for who I was. I cannot remember one day that I did not see Suzanne reading her Bible. I kept asking to read her rule book because I thought the one given to me must have been a Freshman prank, because some of the rules seemed ridiculous. I remember saving our laundry quarters to buy Reese's Pieces Sundaes in the snack shop. I am grateful for a true friend who helped me transition onto the path of maturity.

Day 35

I am grateful for many other friends and roommates that I got to know during college. There was just something about serving and growing together that knitted our hearts together. I am amazed at what some of my friends have gone on to do in serving the Lord. They were then, and are now, encouragements to me in my walk with Him.

Day 36

I am grateful for the many friends with whom I served in the Bus Ministry during college. We prayed together over the lives of the kids we touched. We spent hours on Saturdays trying to change the world. We spent ourselves every Sunday reaching others for Him. We learned so much more because of the opportunities to live out what we were learning. In my heart of hearts I believe the Lord did allow us to change the worlds of at least a few people.

Day 37

I am thankful for my best friend since college, Kristen Hall. We endured World History and Communism class together. We travelled half-way across the country one summer. We have laughed and laughed until we couldn't stop. We shared the heartache of the death of a close friend in our early twenties. We got lost in Indianapolis together. I got lost driving us in Chicago. We have taught many of the same children in different ministries. My friend Kris has encouraged me in my teaching and in my writing. She has been there for me through the ups and downs of two failed engagements. She is a great listener and has the best response for any trial: "I know you will do the right thing." I am truly thankful for my true friend.

Day 38

I can only begin to express my gratitude for those families who treated me {and fed me} like I belonged with them while I was attending college. Tacos and burritos, erros con pollo, attending the Mother-Daughter Banquet with my adopted "Mom and little sisters." Soup and chili on cold Chicago weekends. I truly appreciate these families that have always been so good to me.

Day 39

I am thankful for every child and teenager who rode my bus to church. You helped me to learn and care about others in a way I had not before realized I was capable of doing. I learned from each of you that effective teaching would include so much more than reading, writing, and arithmetic.

Day 40

I am grateful that my parents have always been "for" me. They have given me direction, guidance, love, and support. They have given me decision-making skills and then trusted me to make good decisions. Even when my Mom and Dad have not completely agreed with my decisions they have always shown confidence in me. They reared me to believe that I could do anything that I wanted to do. Anything of any value that I may accomplish I owe to the fact that my parents believed in me.

Day 41

I am so very thankful that my first year's teaching experience was in a small school with understanding parents. I made so many mistakes because of immaturity and/or inexperience. The families that I served chose to see my heart and work with me for the betterment of their child's education to develop the good in me rather than dwell on the mistakes. Surely, each of us could say the same of the beginnings of our careers, whatever the career may be.

Day 42

I am thankful that my first year's teaching experience was in a small school with understanding students. I am glad that the grades were together. We had so much fun; like one, big, extended family! I was so excited to be your teacher! I was thrilled at how much you wanted to learn. I learned so much about teaching, and learning, and life from each of you who called me "Teacher." My teacher, Mrs. Brown once told me that my first class would always hold a special place in my heart. I had no idea just how special.

Day 43

I am grateful that while I was still a young adult the Lord allowed me to serve in ministry with a Preacher and his wife who genuinely cared about the people they were called to Pastor. I observed {up close and personal} midnight hospital runs, tears over the phone, emergency prayer meetings, and many other displays of loving people. I also observed dinner on the grounds, cookouts, birthday parties, their kids having their friends over, and many other displays of enjoying people. I learned so much in those years of being a part of their family, but if I had to condense it all into one statement, it would be this: "We serve God by serving others." I am grateful that I was privileged to learn servant-leadership not in a conference, but in a home.

Day 44

I am thankful for my good friend, one of my first (and one of my favorite students) Regina Bell Lambert. Here is a young lady who was willing to leave her high school and her high school friends in order to attend a Christian school in her Junior year. Her teacher was barely older than her and seriously inexperienced. Somehow, though, we managed to develop a sure and long-lasting friendship. We both really worked at growing into the dual roles of teacher / student and friend / friend. I love you and am so thankful to count you among my true friends. I am thankful that the Lord allowed me to be a part of your life. I am so proud of you for continuing to follow His leading throughout your life.

Day 45: Valentine's Day

In honor of Valentine's Day, this post is slightly out of its chronological order.

I am thankful that I have had the privilege to know what it means to truly be in love. To put the wants and needs of another individual above that of my own. Not at all in the same sense as a child or a young person who NEEDS the adults in their life to do that, but only because I WANTED to. To have another individual love me so much that my wants and needs were put above his own. To sincerely desire to make someone else feel that he is all that matters in the world; and to know he feels the same for me. Yes, I am truly grateful that I know what it means to have loved and lost and can sincerely agree that this is better than never having loved at all.

Day 46

In my life I have given my parents ample opportunities to say, "I told you so." Today I would like to express my gratitude for the fact that they never did. I think that fact has helped me to take ownership of the times they could have better. I am certain that as more age and experience gives me more opportunities to refrain from "I told you so"'s to others I will appreciate this quality more and more.

Day 47

I am thankful for God's unfailing financial provision. I am also grateful that I learned to trust the Lord in this area while I was still a very young adult. I was teaching in Christian School and working part-time at Wal-Mart. I wrote out my budget on paper to see if I could afford a car payment. To my amazement my monthly bills, not including gas and groceries, was $30 MORE than my monthly income! My bills were paid on time and I never missed a meal. I was   -$30 before I even bought groceries, yet the Lord had provided. There have been times in my life when I have worked a regular job and had a little more; there have been times of rice and ramen noodles; but there has never been a time the Lord has not met my needs.   Praise the Lord!!

Day 48

I am grateful for my 1990 Ford Escort. This was the first new car I had ever bought. I prayed and prayed about making a car payment. I wrote out my budget. I had arrived at a payment amount and went to the dealership. I told the salesman what I could afford and asked him to show me only the vehicles in that range. He took me to two Escorts – one with power steering, one without. I could not drive a stick shift, so power steering it was. That vehicle lasted me for many years. It took me to Florida one summer. It moved me to Toledo. It visited my Bus Route with me for hundreds of Saturdays. Yes, I am thankful for my 1990 red Ford Escort.

Day 49

I am thankful for the summer I spent in Tampa with my aunt and uncle. I went with the purpose of tutoring my fourteen-year-old cousin to help prepare him for high school. He was enrolled in a public school which at the time had relegated him to special education classes due to his deafness. He so badly wanted to go to a "regular school" like his brothers. As I said, I went with the purpose of teaching; but I learned *so much.* Michael really worked hard that summer. He learned to read phonetically, even though he could not hear. He learned how to write a book report and diagram sentences. He pushed himself and would not stop until he achieved his personal best. He did go on to a "regular school" for high school. He played on the sports teams and graduated with honors. He also went on to earn his college degree. I am thankful that I learned from my cousin Michael what it means to truly give 110%!

Day 50

I am grateful for Gramma Parson. Here was an older lady at our church who made it her ministry to make sure the younger single ladies did not feel forgotten. She hosted game nights and made us birthday cakes. She cooked Sunday dinners and sent home leftovers. She prayed for and with us. I love and am thankful for older saints who are patient with and care about us young whippersnappers.

Day 51

I am grateful for my dog Zacchaeus. When I brought him home he fit in the palm of my hand. He stayed with me all the time when I was home. He sat on my lap, nipped at my heels, and slept at the foot of my bed. He also grew. Before long, he was waist high and taller than me when his paws were on my shoulders. He still sat in the recliner with me. One time when he jumped on my lap, he toppled the recliner over with me in it! We went for long walks and weekend camping trips with friends and their dogs. I cried and cried when I had to part with Zach! I am thankful for the love of my faithful dog.

Day 52

I am thankful for my good friend Michele. Our hearts were definitely knit over the inner-city kids to whom we ministered through our church. I saw a heart that truly wanted to "mother" these often parentless children. I learned so much from her about reaching others and really listening. I watched my friend sincerely think through, "What Would Jesus Do?" and then try to actually live that way. She loves teaching her First-Graders and truly gives them her heart. I am thankful to say I am a better person for having such a friend as Michele Stephenson.

Day 53

I am thankful for the time I spent at Lewis Avenue Baptist Church serving in the Bus Ministry. I enjoyed teaching and giving to the four and five year old inner city kids. I think working with these boys and girls helped me to see and understand that we are all just people. Neither monetary status nor racial issues mattered to these children. They responded to those of us in their schools and churches whom they felt genuinely cared about them. I grew emotionally and spiritually for the opportunity to work with the inner-city kindergartners of Toledo.

Day 54

I am thankful for "snow days;" a mandated day off. Your school or office is closed. You cannot go to work even if you want to. A day to drink hot chocolate and watch old movies. A day to go sledding or build a snowman. A day to enjoy your friends and family around the old board games. A day to take a nap. Yes, I am truly grateful for unexpected "snow days."

Day 55

I am grateful that I was able to be home with my Mom during her final months on this earth. I am thankful that she wanted me to be. I am thankful that when the hospice nurse said that it was time for my brother and me to make amends with our mother that we could truthfully say there was nothing between us. I miss my Mom tremendously. I am grateful that she taught us to have no regrets. I am grateful that my Mom is no longer in any pain. I really miss her, but I am grateful that I will see my Mom again someday.

Day 56

I am grateful for all of our friends and family who came to see my Mom during her final battle with cancer. I am grateful for her demonstration of faith, strength, and bravery during this time. My Mom called her friends and family to tell them there would be no funeral after her passing. She asked them to please come to see her and let her say "good-bye." I could (and probably should) write an entire book on the things I learned from my mother. This demonstration of faith and courage in the face of certain and painful death may have been among the greatest. I love and miss my Mom. I am grateful for others who loved her also.

Day 57

Our society does not value words in the same sense as we once did. People often say things with little or no thought as to what they actually mean. I am grateful that my parents taught us not to say things that we do not mean. I am thankful that my parents taught me the importance of words, especially words that may be the last words someone will hear from your lips. "I love you" are the last words my family says to each other and others that we love when leaving them, or hanging up the phone. I am grateful that the last words my Mom and I said to each other were "I love you."

Day 58

People occasionally debate whether it is easier to lose someone slowly or to lose someone suddenly. My response would be that it is never easy to lose someone. Today, though, I would like to say that I am thankful that my Mom's last words to her family were "Good bye. I love you." It was not at all easy to watch my Mom battle cancer twice. It was definitely not easy to see her die. But she knew she was leaving and wanted us to be happy for her journey. Just as I wanted her to be happy for me when I left for college. Just as my brother wanted her to be happy for him at his wedding. She had the same excitement and anticipation as we all experience when preparing for a trip or a new chapter in our lives. She knew that she would soon be with the Lord. I am thankful that my Mom was able to tell us "Good bye" before she passed from this world into the next.

Day 59

On February 28, 1981, I asked Jesus Christ to come into my heart, forgive my sin and take me to Heaven someday when I die. I trusted His death on the cross and the fact that He rose again from the dead to pay my penalty for sin. I am thankful that Jesus always says "yes" to those who call upon His name. Today, I am truly grateful for God's free gift of salvation.

please see epilogue for more information regarding this decision

March

Day 60

I am grateful for the years the Lord allowed me to teach preschool. I learned so much about patience and fairness. I learned the importance of hugs and kisses. I learned the power of the time-out and I learned the power of the nap. Immediately after my Mom's death I had a job that daily consisted of three- and four- year-olds sitting on my lap telling me they loved me. The Lord knew exactly what I needed to help me through a very difficult time.

Day 61

I am grateful for the other preschool teachers with whom I worked. I believe these ladies are often overlooked in the world, even in church ministries. For little pay, often even less than the Christian school teacher, these ladies form the characters of our future leaders. They impart a sense of value to our future young people. I believe at the Judgement Seat we may all be a little surprised at the importance of the roles of the "Day-Care Ladies."

Day 62 *This entry refers to "Mr. Freeze" in Perrysburg, Ohio.*

"I scream, you scream; we all scream for ice cream!" I am grateful for the Perrysburg Ice Cream Store! I love ice cream! This ice cream store tops them all with their toppings. This is the first place I ever had a peanut butter / marshmallow milkshake. This is the first place I ever had a pineapple / coconut milkshake. I have many memories of Saturday field trips to the Perrysburg Ice Cream Store, and every one of them are good memories!

Day 63

I am thankful for daily devotionals and yearly Bible reading schedules. Sometimes life gets busy; problems and stressful situations seem to take over. Without a plan or a guide my Bible reading and prayer time seems to lessen. Usually during those times I should seek God's face more, I have a tendency to squeeze His time out. Having a devotional book and / or a daily guide has done much to help me keep my devotional life on track. While living in Toledo I started reading the One Year Bible which has a portion of OT, NT, a Psalm, and a chapter of Proverbs each day. Since then I have also enjoyed Sarah Young's *Jesus Calling* series and various selections by Max Lucado.

Day 64

I am thankful for my friends Rich and Lori Havey. I am thankful for the times they loaned me their car, cooked or grilled dinner, picked me up or dropped me off at the airport. I am also grateful for all the time they allowed me to spend with their girls. The previous entries about taking walks in the woods or driving to Perrysburg for ice cream almost always included one or both of their girls. I am grateful for a family that treated me like family while I lived in Toledo. I really miss my friend Lori.

Day 65

I am thankful for young people who decide to follow the Lord's leading in their lives regardless of what obstacles they may have to overcome. Christy Havey is one such young person. She served on the Bus Route and in Kindergarten Junior Church throughout her teen years. She graduated from high school and went on to Bible College. After graduating from Bob Jones University she worked at their radio station for several years. Upon moving back to Toledo, she served as a volunteer teacher's aide for several years. In case you don't already know, I should mention that Christy accomplished all of this without being able to see. Christy was born with severely impaired vision and has been legally blind since birth. Her sister April, also legally blind, has a similar story and extraordinary character. Yes, I am thankful that there are young people who pursue their dreams and goals regardless of the obstacles.

Day 66

I spent a lot of time walking the Luna Pier along Lake Erie. It was calm and peaceful there. Sometimes there were fishermen, sometimes young couples, sometimes older people just thinking. Sometimes I was alone; often times, not. Sometimes we took a picnic; sometimes we just talked; sometimes I just prayed. There is something about the water that calms my heart. I am thankful for Luna Pier along the shoreline of Lake Erie.

Day 67

I am thankful for the teen girls who came early to Sunday night church to listen to Michele and me talk about the Lord. Preparing something to talk about that would be both relevant and hopefully interesting to them taught us so much about walking with the Lord. Being Christ like truly is so much more about a relationship with Him than anything else. Our outward appearance gradually changes as our inward being reflects Him. I am thankful for each of these ladies who wanted more from life than the world had to offer.

Day 68

I am thankful for doctors who take the time to listen to their patients. While living in Toledo I had a doctor who helped me treat my migraines. She asked questions and listened to the answers. She helped me find a medication that treated the cause of the headaches rather than just than symptoms. I have found such a doctor here in Hot Springs also, but thankfully, she has not had to treat me for severe migraines. I am thankful for modern medicine; but I am also thankful for caring and sympathetic medical personnel.

Day 69

I am grateful for the convenience of flight. I am thankful that I can go to the airport and within a few hours be with my family in a different state. I could join with many others and disparage the TSA who sometimes seem to be going out of their way to make the convenience of flight more and more inconvenient; but the truth is, I am also grateful for the safety of flight. I am thankful for how easy it is to coordinate a visit with my family and I need to take advantage of it more often.

Day 70

I am thankful for Bambino's on Eleanor Street {in Toledo}. I am sure that I took advantage of the pizza parlor directly across the street from my house much more than I should have! They made the best meatball subs ~ nothing like Subway's. Their food tasted authentically Italian! For $1 extra they would deliver. Usually we would just walk over and pick it up; but during a Toledo snowstorm, delivery was well worth $2. Oh yes, I am grateful for the period of time I lived across the street from Bambino's.

Day 71

I am thankful for the experience of having been to Europe. I have seen the London Bridge and Buckingham Palace. I have sat atop a double-decker bus. I have seen "Phantom of the Opera" in Her Majesty's Theatre in London. I have seen a Shakespearean play at The Royal Shakespearean Theatre at Stratford on Avon. I have been to the Louvre and seen the Mona Lisa and the Venus de Milo. I have been to the top of the Eiffel Tower. And, best of all, I got to experience all of this with one of my closest and dearest lifetime friends.

Day 72

I am thankful for answered prayers. I remember praying for an entire year for a van to provide transportation for the young people to attend church youth activities, Saturday visitation, and trips to the Perrysburg Ice Cream Store. My friend Michele picked me up from the airport after Christmas vacation driving the answer to our prayers. Her parents had bought a car, but the salesman had mixed up the paperwork and given them a van instead. They got a real bargain on it because the car had already been sold to someone else. They traded the van to my friend for her compact car. And that's not all – a family in our church put the key to their van in a Christmas card for me to open on the way home. They needed a larger van and the Lord had led them to give theirs to me rather than sell or trade it. Praise the Lord!! He had given us two vans! We tried our best to use and fill them for and with young people for His glory!

Day 73

I am thankful for coffee! I love the smell of it. I love the taste of it (with a little creamer). I love its "wake me up" feeling. I am thankful for plain, cheap coffee. I am thankful for flavored coffee. I am thankful for Dunkin Donuts coffee. I am thankful for Starbucks. I am thankful for WaWa Coffee. I was especially thankful for coffee on cold Toledo winter mornings.

Day 74

I am thankful for the hymns of the faith and songs of praise. I love music and I especially love music that brings glory to the Lord. I love to hear people sing and / or play an instrument. Being unable to carry a tune that remotely resembles any song makes me even more appreciative of those who practice and learn the songs to be a blessing and encouragement to others. I am thankful for uplifting tapes and cds I have had throughout the years. I am thankful that Scripture asks of us a "joyful noise" and not a "beautifully arranged melody."

Day 75

I am thankful for good books. During one of those Toledo summers I read my friend Kristen's collection of classics. Having grown up with Nancy Drew, my attention was first drawn to Sherlock Holmes. Then Dickens, then Tennyson, then Hawthorne. I read all of the classics that summer. I re-read "The Chronicles of Narnia," another childhood favorite. I enjoy and am thankful for good books.

Day 76

I am thankful for my health. I have already mentioned my Mom's battles with cancer and as I am typing this, two people very close to me have been affected by cancer this year. So many people have physical ailments or afflictions and persevere through life in spite of it. I am grateful for their example. I am so very thankful that thus far in my life I have been blessed with good health.

Day 77

I am grateful for Teen Soulwinning programs. Here is an opportunity for young people to develop their leadership skills in a spiritual arena. It is a good thing for our young people to develop the boldness and people skills necessary to share their faith with others. I am grateful for the time I spent as an adult sponsor of Teen Soulwinning.

Day 78

I am thankful for odd jobs that help supplement my main income. In Toledo, two of my friends had paper routes and I occasionally helped. Another family placed door hangers with advertisements and coupons and many of us would help "stuff" every Thursday. I have worked after school at Wal-Mart and Cracker Barrel. There is always babysitting. I am thankful that money is available for "extras" when we are willing to work for it.

Day 79

I am thankful for and truly miss Friday night game nights. A bunch of us girls would get together and play Clue or Monopoly or cards. Gramma Parson would have something good for us to eat, or we would order a pizza. We laughed and played and shared highlights from our week. We talked about "men" in our lives and our plans for the future. We just had fun on Friday nights.

Day 80

I am grateful for the internet. And Google. And iPhones. And Syrie. And all the other things that sprang from the internet that make our lives so much easier. Sometimes I think we are guilty of taking modern technology for granted. My grandparents grew up without indoor plumbing and we have home wifi. We often forget just how far we have come and just how good we have it. Even as I write this I am preparing to move to the mission field and I know I can keep in touch with my friends and family because of the internet. Phone calls, e-mails, and even face-time are inexpensively available to me.

Day 81

I am thankful for the Bus Ministry and those with whom I have served in it. I am thankful for faithful Bus Captains and Bus Workers who give their weekends to the mission fields that are their hometowns. I am thankful for those who give financially that the busses may continue to run. I am thankful for Pastors who keep this ministry in front of their congregations as a tangible way to serve and reach others. I am thankful for the Sunday School Teachers who love and work with the young people who are brought to Jesus through the Bus Ministry. I am tremendously grateful for the Bus Ministry and all of the blessings God has brought to my life through it.

Day 82

I am thankful for comfortable shoes. Especially tennis shoes. But also, shoes that are dressy without too much of a heel. Shoes that look nice without giving a constant reminder to your feet that you are dressed up. Such shoes are not easily found and are greatly mourned when they wear out.

Day 83

I am thankful that Jenny was able to learn to play the violin at Start High School in Toledo. If this were the only reason God had (and I do not believe it was) for her to attend public school, it would have been worth it. I have always loved to hear her play. I enjoyed the concerts and recitals. I am so glad for the opportunities I had to drive to regional competitions and statewide performances. I still enjoy listening to her play. I am thrilled that she is able to teach it to others. I am truly grateful for all the hours that were put in to her mastery of a musical instrument.

Day 84

I am grateful for nature hikes. While I was living in Toledo my friends and I walked through Wildwood Forest for hours at a time. We would watch for rabbits and deer. We would listen for the birds and try to name them. We would admire the unusual flowers and plants. For the most part we avoided the poison ivy. I really enjoy walking outside with no agenda or time frame. (Note that none of us owned a cell phone at this time.) I am grateful for nature and the closeness that can be developed with God as well as those with whom you are walking.

Day 85 Spring Break

I am thankful for Spring Break! A whole free week smack dab in the middle of winter and summer to do whatever you want. Sleep in. Plan a trip. Visit a relative. Bake cookies. Do something special with the kids. A whole free week.

Day 86

One year for my birthday all of my friends in Toledo went together and bought me a Franklin Day Planner. I loved it! I took it with me everywhere and wrote down all of my appointments and special occasions. I still use planners; just a little less expensive ones. I am thankful for calendars and day planners. And I am thankful that my friends took time to make me feel special and appreciated on my special day.

Day 87

While on the theme of birthdays I must single out my "surprise" birthday party. Since my birthday is in December and the party was in August, I must admit that it was a true surprise! You see, my previous birthday, my 30th, I had spent with my Mom during her final struggle with cancer. So when I returned to Toledo, my friends wanted me to know that they had not forgotten me. We went to the park and had lots of food and ice cream. I am thankful for friends and birthdays.

Day 88 Easter Week / Palm Sunday

On Palm Sunday we pause to remember Jesus' triumphal entry into Jerusalem. Many of the people thought He was coming to free them from Roman oppression. The freedom offered through Jesus is more a freedom from one's self than a freedom from oppression by others. Just as we find today, many people were confused by this. Many desire a more tangible, less intangible god. Even the religious people desire a more emotional, less spiritual experience. I am grateful that one day Jesus will be crowned King of Kings and Lord of Lords. Until that day, may I daily recognize Him as the King of my heart.

Day 89 Easter Week

My Mom loved Easter! She would make and hide Easter Baskets for my brother and me every year, even after we were grown up. She would fill these baskets with candy, especially jelly beans, baseball cards, and other little things she thought we might enjoy. The baskets could be hidden anywhere throughout the house. One Easter Sunday I discovered mine in the shower! We were not allowed to tell if we found the one that was not ours. I am thankful that my Mom always looked for special ways to show her love for us.

Day 90 Easter Week

I am grateful that at least once in my life I have experienced a Jewish Seder, which is the celebration of the Passover. Every item of the meal had significance to those partaking. Every item of the meal also had a corresponding significance to the Passover week which Jesus experienced in the New Testament. It is amazing to me how much detail is presented and preserved in the fulfilling of prophecy. I am grateful that I was allowed to partake of this sacred Jewish tradition and observe the relevance it has to New Testament Christianity.

April

Day 91 Easter Week

I am thankful that at least once in my life I have been a part of an Easter sunrise service. To imagine what Mary must have felt when she first saw the empty tomb. To think of the disciples racing each other to see for themselves what Mary had already described. The experience of an Easter sunrise service could only be surpassed by actually being in Jerusalem.

Day 92 Easter Week

I remember shopping for Easter outfits as a little girl. I would get a bright colorful dress and my brother would get a new suit with a (usually blue) pastel tie. Almost everyone I knew would get a new outfit during this week. But the excitement was not just about the clothes. The new "springy" outfits were just a picture of the newness of life that comes with spring, and especially with Easter. I am thankful for the excitement of Spring that surrounds the Easter holiday!

Day 93 Easter Week / Good Friday

I realize that there are some scholars who believe that Jesus died on a Wednesday. I will not argue that point. However, most Christian denominations recognize today as "Good Friday." The crucifixion was actually an extremely dark and ominous event. On that particular day one would be hard pressed to find even one thing good. Those who had forsaken all and followed Christ closely for the previous three years now forsook Him and fled. So why do we call this day "Good Friday?" Because everything in our spiritual lives that we recognize as Good was made possible because of the events of this day.

"But He was wounded for our transgressions, He was bruised for our iniquities: the chastisement of our peace was upon Him; and with His stripes we are healed." ~ Is. 53:6 KJV.

Day 94 Easter Week

I remember Easter egg hunts as a child. My Gramma made them extra fun with candy and sometimes coins inside the eggs. Each of us cousins had our own particular color of plastic egg. The younger we were, the easier our color was to find. Yes, I am thankful for the coming holiday and all that it means; as well as all of the fun that comes with celebrating it.

Day 95 Easter Week / Easter Sunday

Today we celebrate the most important story in the Bible; the very reason we have a Bible. Today we celebrate the single most important event in all of History – the Resurrection of Jesus from the dead. The empty tomb and the promise that He will come again. I am thankful not only for this event, but also for the fact that I live in a nation that still celebrates this holiday. Yes, I am thankful for Easter and all that it means; and all that it means to me.

Day 96

New York! New York! I am truly thankful that I have had the opportunity to visit the city that never sleeps. I have seen the Statue of Liberty and Ellis Island. I have enjoyed an off-Broadway play. I have ridden the subway through the five boroughs. I have walked across the Brooklyn Bridge. My good friend Kristen and I had so much fun on this trip. I am thankful that her Uncle Paul let us stay with him during our visit. I am thankful to her Nana for our steaks at Donovan's. I am truly thankful that I have experienced New York City.

Day 97

I am thankful that I have seen both the Atlantic and Pacific Oceans. I have put my feet in and taken pictures. I have tasted the salty brine of both coasts. There is something both majestic and peaceful about the ocean. I love to hear the waves smack the shore. I love to smell the air and feel the sea breeze. I like the feel of squishing sand between my toes. I am thankful to have experienced the sea coasts.

Day 98

I am thankful for microwave ovens. I am glad I can put a meal of leftovers on the same plate and heat them up in two or three minutes. Some of us can remember leftovers involving numerous pots, plates, and lids. I remember when our family first got a microwave. My brother and I cooked two pounds of bacon just to watch it shrink up while it quickly cooked. We got in BIG trouble! I appreciate the convenience of the microwave oven.

Day 99

Washing dishes was my job growing up. Most of the time Mom and I did them together. Sunday dinners at Grandma's, Thanksgiving and Christmas, my cousin Lisa and I completed the task of washing, drying, and cleaning the tables and stove. These are the reasons for which I am very grateful for the dishwasher.

Day 100

While living in Toledo I worked for a few years at a chiropractor's office, consequently experiencing my first chiropractic adjustment. "Optimum Health" he called it. Honestly, I felt fine and did not really think an adjustment would affect me at all. Was I ever wrong! I am so very grateful for chiropractors and their knowledge of how to help hurting patients as well as make those in good health feel even better.

Day 101

I also worked for a dentist within the same medical corporation as the chiropractor. Though I had been to a dentist before I am not sure if I could have truthfully said I was thankful for this profession until this time. I am grateful for those whose purpose in life is to heal the broken tooth and cure or prevent gum disease. If you have ever truly needed one, I am certain you can join me in being grateful for the dentist.

Day 102

I am thankful for faithful Pastors. I have mentioned a few of my previous Pastors. Dr. Les Hobbins of Lewis Avenue Baptist Church, Temperance, Michigan, was my Pastor during this period of my life. I can only remember a handful of Sundays in the seven years I was a member that Pastor Hobbins was not there. I have been privileged to have a Biblically founded New Testament Church in which to worship and serve wherever I have lived. I am grateful for these God-fearing men and their wives who have given their lives to provide Spiritual building blocks for the rest of us to use in building our lives. Won't you take a moment with me today and be thankful for your Pastor and Pastor's Wife?

Day 103

I am thankful for mystery novels and movies – the good old "Whodunit?" I have previously mentioned books in general, but I am referring to the suspense that makes my neck hairs bristle wondering what is going to happen next. From *Nancy Drew* to Agatha Christie and Mary Higgins Clark; from *Murder She Wrote* and *Diagnosis Murder* to *Law and Order, NCIS,* and *Criminal Intent,* to the great mystery movies of Alfred Hitchcock and other classics; I truly enjoy trying to piece the clues together and solve the mystery. Sometimes I am right and sometimes I am wrong. I just enjoy the thrill of the chase from the safety of the sofa.

Day 104

I love the smell and feel of clean warm towels right out of the dryer! I love to fall asleep on freshly cleaned sheets! When I was a kid my Mom continued to hang the sheets out on the line even after we could afford a dryer because we all loved the "fresh air scent." I am thankful for household washers and dryers and I am thankful for fresh clean linens.

Day 105 April 15 -- Tax Day

April 15! Tax Day! Ugh, we all like to complain about paying taxes. However, I am grateful for so many things that we often take for granted in America: highway systems, institutions of higher learning, police and fire departments, the military. I am sure we could add many more things that our tax dollars fund for which we should be thankful.

{Disclaimer: I do believe the current tax system could use a major overhaul.}

Day 106

Handwritten notes and cards have become a scarcity in our technological age. I love to get "snail-mail." Christmas cards, birthday cards, just because cards; thank-you notes and "thinking of you" notes. I try to include a personal, hand-written sentiment when I send a card. Even when posting a digital greeting, I try to say something personal. I am thankful for heart-felt, especially handwritten, notes.

Day 107

Games. Today I am thankful for games. Monopoly, Clue, Trouble, Life, Sorry, Uno, Card Games. Every Saturday that we could not play outside found me and my cousins playing board games at Gramma's. Growing up, everyone on my end of the block would alternate hosting card games. The grown-ups played at the kitchen table while the kids could be found in the den or the basement. Hearts, Spades, Pinochle, Peanuts. I love to play games.

Day 108

I am thankful for pictures. When I left the first school at which I had ever taught I was gifted with an album of memories which I still cherish. I have an album for each of the trips I have enjoyed. I treasure family pictures and school yearbooks. I have class pictures of my students that span a quarter of a century. I am thankful for these images and the oh-so-many memories they represent.

Day 109

I am thankful for the Sunday Funnies! When I lived in Toledo I got the paper every day from my friends who had paper routes. I loved reading the comics. I especially loved reading them on Sundays. It is a nice chuckle, the original LOL moments. I love *Peanuts* and *Garfield; Cathy* and *The Far Side.* I used to read them out loud on the Sunday School Bus sometimes. I love a good laugh and I always get one when reading the Sunday Funnies.

Day 110

On my last day in Toledo, which happened to be Halloween and Old Fashioned Sunday, my Dad bought Pizza for everyone on my church-bus. We had a big party. Dad had had driven down to help me move my things to Arkansas. All my friends hugged me and wished me well after the evening church service. Dad met many of them and thanked them for their roles in my life. On Monday morning, we loaded up our cars and headed South. I am grateful to my father for ALWAYS supporting me in my life decisions; for tangibly supporting these decisions. Whether or not he has completely agreed with me, my Dad has always completely believed in me. I love and am thankful for my Dad and his help in moving to Arkansas.

Day 111

If you know me at all, you have heard plenty of humorous "Only in Arkansas" sayings or stories from me. But today, I would like to be thankful for so many positives that are "Only in Arkansas" things. I have never heard a story about violent road rage in Arkansas. I think that is because no one is ever in a hurry. At least, not that much of a hurry. Here, people still stop on the road to "howdy" with their neighbors. People still have their friends over for dinner. High School sporting events are more popular than professional ones. Strangers will stop to help you change your tire. The well water is often the same as the rest of the country's bottled water (mine was Mountain Valley Spring Water; but also think Ozarka). Lost wallets or credit cards are more likely to be returned than stolen. The general populace still believe in and fear God and have a respect for His house; even if they admittedly do not frequent it often enough. Local politics are still important. I am so very grateful for every day of the fifteen plus years I have been a citizen of Arkansas.

Day 112

Although I certainly did not feel thankful at the time, I am thankful that First Grade was the only teaching position available at the school when I moved. I thought I wanted to teach High School ... but, I fell in love not only with the students that year, but also with witnessing the firsts of First Grade. The "aha moments" when children realize they can read! When adding and subtracting suddenly make sense! I loved to see them first understand Bible stories and historical events. I truly loved and enjoyed teaching First Grade!

Day 113

I am eternally grateful to the parents of my first few First Grade classes in Arkansas. It took some getting used to for both of us. I was adjusting to Arkansas culture as you were trying to adjust to your "babies" becoming "big-kids." I loved your children. I truly loved being their teacher. So today, I am grateful that you gave me room to grow into the teacher that you wanted your kids to have. Thank you for accepting me and taking the time to get to know me. Thank you for allowing me to help you teach your children.

Day 114

I am thankful for the privilege of teaching and influencing young people who are or soon will be the leaders of their generation. I have been honored to be called "Teacher" by some truly amazing young people. I strove to help give them firm foundations on which to build their lives. And build they have and are! This is not only true of those here in Arkansas; but I believe that it was here that I felt overwhelmed with the responsibility of what I was imparting to these now young adults who would one day shape the direction and values of our communities, our churches, and our nation.

Day 115

I am grateful for phone calls to friends and family. These originally started on Saturdays for me because of free long-distance on the weekends. Of course, now most cell phones include nationwide coverage. I enjoy connecting with those who are important to me and to whom I am important. I am thankful for the ability to "catch up" with a phone call.

Day 116

I am thankful for Sunday afternoon naps. It is something to look forward to all week. I especially like to take mine on the couch. I feel like I am sneaking extra sleep. It is nice once in the week to have nothing pressing in on the schedule; a time to just lay back and relax.

Day 117

Have I mentioned how good the food is in Arkansas? Oh boy, am I thankful for good, down-home cooking! So many friends have had me over for dinner or "get-togethers" that have always included great food. Sunday dinner was always an invitation to covet! Sweet-Tea, Bar-B-Que, chili, homemade soups, steaks or burgers on the grill, grilled vegetables, "real" mashed potatoes with home-made gravy, slow baked ham . . . And the desserts!! Oh, the desserts!!!!

Day 118

Several friends have come to visit me here in Arkansas. I appreciate their taking the time to leave their world and spend a few days in mine. It makes others feel special and important when for a brief time the world does revolve around them. Even a card or a phone call can be such a source of encouragement. I am sure we could each think of at least one someone today who needs a little extra attention from us. I am especially grateful to those who came to visit me during the summer of 2007: the wedding was cancelled, but our friendship was strengthened.

Day 119

Nothing feels better after a hard day's work than a hot shower. I am thankful for this luxury that we tend to take for granted in America. The dirt washes away and we are left looking, feeling, and smelling better.

Day 120

I am thankful for camp outs and fishing trips on Lake Ouchita. These were usually enjoyed with the Perrymans and various other friends in Arkansas. One summer I was the "Queen of the Innertube!" I held on to the rope longer than anybody, even the teenagers. The title was short-lived, but at least it was once achieved. I usually played in the water with the kids while others were grilling or fishing or just talking by the water's edge. I truly appreciate a lazy summer's day spent at the lake.

May

Day 121

I am thankful for dependable transportation. I am thankful to be able to drive to work, to church, to the store, wherever I want to go. I am thankful for the independence and freedom I enjoy as the direct result of owning a vehicle. Every time I have needed a vehicle, the Lord has provided one. For most of my adult life my Dad has bought and personally fixed up a car and brought it to me wherever I was living at the time. The few times I have purchased a vehicle, it has been extremely evident that the Lord was providing it.

Day 122

At one time in my life, I was without a vehicle for several weeks. One of my friends asked if I knew yet what I was going to do about getting a car. I wish I could say I answered prayerfully, or even nicely. After a few minutes I replied with a rather scornful tone: "God is not going to just open the sky and send a car floating down out of Heaven!" At that exact moment, a parent of children in our Christian school came over to the playground and asked if he had correctly heard from the other parents that I was in need of a vehicle? His work had provided one for him and he and his wife each already had one. Would I like to drive the Saturn or the Mercedes? Sometimes God provides for our needs to prove that He can. I am thankful that even at times when my heart is not completely in the right spot, God is always in time on time every time for me.

Day 123

I am grateful for good Christian fellowship. I enjoy the meet-and-greet times before and after church. I especially enjoy special Sunday night fellowships after services that involve eating. I enjoy the hand-shaking time during the service. I am grateful for good Christian fellowship.

Day 124

I am truly grateful for my glasses. It is amazing how clear the world becomes when these amazing frames are placed over my ears. I can read clearly and drive more safely. Sometimes it even seems I can think more deeply because of my glasses.

Day 125

I am truly grateful for bosses who make their employees feel noticed and appreciated. For oh-so-many years of teaching First Grade I would announce to my little charges why I loved that particular day. One year on Tuesdays they always knew because I was usually still holding my coffee as we lined up. Our acting principal that year had arranged with our college coffee shop to pay for all the teachers' drinks every Tuesday. That gesture of appreciation made me want to come to school early. It helped my frame of mind as I entered the classroom. It felt nice to be appreciated.

Day 126

When I would announce why I loved Wednesdays, my favorite week-day, my little First-Graders already knew why. I loved Pee Wee Patch! For several years our church used Ron Hamilton's guides for Scripture memory and character development through his Patch the Pirate series. During Wednesday night church, I taught the four to six year old class called Pee Wee Patch. It was an excellent program and I thoroughly enjoyed teaching it. I had several parent helpers who commented to me that they always learned something from the lessons as well. I am grateful for any program that builds character through Scripture into the next generation. I am just a little partial to the Patch Programs.

Day 127

I also love AfterCare! (after-school care). I got to hear all about the school day from the kids' point of view. I always asked what was the most exciting part of their day. Sometimes during snack time I would pretend I wasn't listening and they would just talk about their lessons and friends and what happened at recess. I enjoyed helping the students lick that long-division problem or help them diagram their sentences. I really do love AfterCare. I am going to miss it when I move.

Day 128

I am thankful for talk radio. It helps me fall asleep at night. Seriously, though, I am thankful for the freedom of speech we enjoy in America that allows various people from various walks of life with various political and religious views to air their opinions for anyone willing to listen. Sometimes I am informed, sometimes amused, sometimes outraged. And sometimes I am thankful for the freedom to change the station.

Day 129

I am thankful for Scott and Lisa Perryman who have been more than family to me. They have fed me, fixed my cars, changed my tires, and killed many critters for me. Lisa and I have laughed, cried, and prayed together. I have had the privilege of influencing their three boys. Lisa promised me on the day I moved to Arkansas that she and her family would be my family in Arkansas. I am thankful that she has more than kept that promise. The Perrymans are so good to so many people. I am grateful to God for them and their kindness to me and others.

Day 130

I am grateful for churches who place a special emphasis on bringing visitors: contests, seasonal programs, pushes and prizes. I appreciate churches who make a visitor feel welcome and comfortable. It does not matter how you got there or what you are wearing; it only matters that you chose to worship the Lord with us this morning. Praise the Lord for inclusive Scriptural worship of our Saviour!

Day 131 The Senses

"Oh, be careful little eyes what you see." It is an amazing thing to be able to see. As we study the intricate machinations of our eyes we learn that something so simple as seeing is actually a rather complicated undertaking. Even when we enjoy videoes or pictures we are only enjoying a feeble attempt to reproduce God's creation known as the eye. I am thankful for my eyes.

Day 132 The Senses

"Oh, be careful little ears what you hear." It is an amazing thing to be able to hear. It is even more amazing to me that we are able to differentiate subtle differences that allow us to distinguish the voices of our loved ones; even more than that, to be able to interpret their meanings. A mother does not just hear that her baby is crying; she immediately knows whether it is hungry or hurt or anxious. I am thankful for my ears.

Day 133 The Senses

Is there a certain aroma that makes you think of home? Can you remember your mom's perfume? I enjoy the different smells associated with the seasons. The smell of homemade biscuits. Fresh coffee. Donuts. Lilacs. Babies. Breakfast. Outdoor cookouts. I am thankful for my sense of smell.

Day 134 The Senses

Do you remember in grade school learning where the sweet / salty / bitter taste buds are located on your tongue? Do you remember the teacher bringing lemons, salt, and sugar for experimenting? I love the taste of saltwater at the ocean. I love the taste of honeysuckle fresh from the vine. I love the taste of coffee. I am thankful that God allows us to enjoy the food we eat with different tastes.

Day 135 The Senses

"Oh, be careful little tongue what you say." Our tongue allows us to talk as well as taste. I am thankful that I can communicate with words. I can ask for help and I can give encouragement. I can show appreciation and I can say "You're welcome." I can ask for directions and I can offer guidance. God tells us in James that "death and life are in the power of the tongue." I am thankful for words of thoughtfulness and encouragement, given and received.

Day 136 The Senses

Smooth or rough, silky or cotton, it is an amazing thing to feel with our skin. It is comforting to hold the hand of one we love. We feel our way through a darkened room. We can feel a cool breeze or a fevered brow. We can wipe away the tears of a child or smooth his unruly hair. I am also grateful for our sense of touch.

Day 137 The Senses

I am grateful for the feeling of conviction when the sermon steps on my toes. I am glad the Lord still talks to me through the preaching of His Word. May the Lord help me to respond properly when He pricks my heart.

Day 138 The Senses

"Oh, be careful little hands what you do." Our hands are powerful tools. Who we are on the inside determines what we choose to do with our hands. Builders build. Farmers farm. Teachers teach. Healers heal. Writers write. I am thankful for my hands and the ability to earn my way through life by using them for the betterment of myself and others.

Day 139 The Senses

"Oh, be careful little feet where you go." I have visited a lot of different places on the earth in the years I have spent here. I have also experienced numerous places of life. I have been on the mountaintop; I have been in the valley. I have experienced the sunshine and the rain; the thunderclaps as well as the rainbow. My feet have carried me, literally and figuratively to each place. I am thankful for my feet and all the places they have taken me.

Day 140

For several summers in Arkansas I ran a summer week-day program for children while their parents were working. The local library sponsored several fun educational events. I planned out some fun activities and field trips. We would have lunch at the park or pool where we could play or swim. I had so much fun those summers that I almost felt guilty charging a fee. I am thankful for the parents who allowed me to enjoy summer vacation with their children, and for the children who enjoyed it with me.

Day 141

I am also thankful for friends who let me swim in their pools in the evenings after the children went home. Sometimes with friends, sometimes alone; but always relaxing. I love to swim and am so grateful for those willing to share the blessing that is a swimming pool.

Day 142

I am grateful for coloring books. When I was little, my Mom and I used to color together. We would imagine that we were "in the picture" and make up adventures to share. I enjoy the quiet that ensues when otherwise noisy children are given pages and colors. I like to use a coloring page with the Sunday School Lesson. I am thankful for coloring books.

Day 143

I am also thankful for crayons. Especially Crayola crayons from Hallmark; especially the Sixty-four box! It was a great day when we got that giant box of colors as kids. There was no limit to what we could create! I enjoy watching children now when they open a box of sixty-four crayons. They eagerly, yet carefully choose a color for each part of the picture. I am thankful for the color that children bring into our lives.

Day 144

I am grateful for the truly Southern event known as Sunday Dinner. As a young person these were often enjoyed at Grandma's house. Sometimes my Mom would put the pot roast in the crock pot with potatoes and carrots and flour gravy. (That is still my favorite!) Many times as a single adult, I have been invited to the home of others to enjoy this tradition. For many years, the Perrymans would have many of us over after our bus routes. I am truly thankful for Sunday Dinner.

Day 145 Patriorism / Memorial Day

Memorial Day was originally deemed "Remembrance Day." A day set aside for our whole nation to remember and be thankful for those who stand in the gap and make up the hedge in defense of our freedom. I am thankful for every man and woman who has given up their freedoms for a period of time and has been willing to lay down their lives to preserve the freedoms I enjoy.

Day 146

I am grateful for all of the parents who supported me in the opening of my own educational services business. I also appreciate my friends and family who supported me financially in this endeavor. I enjoy one-on-one learning. I loved teaching small classes on the junior High level. I appreciate the trust and confidence you demonstrated by allowing me to influence your young person. I am grateful for the period of time in my life that I enjoyed being a small business owner.

Day 147

Although chronologically sooner than business owner, I am also grateful that for a period of time I have been a homeowner. It was nice to have a place carved out of the mountain that was all mine and only mine. Literally carved. It is nice to have a refuge from the grit and grime of life. It was a little place of refreshing and rest. I especially appreciate my neighbors who were so good to me at this time.

Day 148

I am thankful for central heat and air. At times I find myself taking amenities such as this for granted. However, in just a few short weeks I will find myself where central air is not. Many more places in our world operate without central heat and air than places that enjoy the luxury. It is nice to be able to change a setting and stay warm in the winter and cool in the summer.

Day 149

I have not often publicly expressed my gratitude for Jenny. Here is an amazing young lady who once decided to allow the Lord to make something beautiful of her life. To my knowledge, she is the only graduate of Start High School in Toledo to attend Bible College. She married a missionary, spent numerous years sleeping in hotels or other people's houses while on deputation, adjusted to a new culture in a new country, worked tediously to master a second language, and is rearing three children to love and honor God. And she truly considers herself humbly honored to be chosen for all of these tasks. I am truly grateful for my friend, Jenny.

Day 150 Creation

I am thankful that God has chosen to give us light and darkness. I am thankful for bright, sunny days and I am thankful for dark, quiet nights. I am thankful for the good times in life; and I am thankful for the darker times that teach me to draw closer to Him. I am thankful for bright, happy days; and I am thankful for dark, gloomy nights. Most of all, I am thankful that God is the same regardless of what I can or cannot see.

Day 151 Creation

I am thankful for the seas and the sky. I love the water: ponds and lakes, creeks and rivers, oceans and seas. I enjoy wading through creeks or at the edge of the ocean. I like to just stick my feet in the water. I love the sky. Whether lying on my back looking up or seated on a plane looking out, I love to watch the clouds float along through the skies. I like to pick out shapes or characters among the clouds. The seas and sky remind us of the limitless possibilities of the God we serve. I am thankful for the seas and the sky.

June

Day 152 Creation

I am thankful for the land and the trees, the flowers and the grass, the dirt and the soil. I am thankful for the variety of vegetation that can be found on our planet. I love fruits and vegetables. I enjoy peanuts and walnuts and pecans. Flowers are always a pleasing gift whether from an admirer or a little child. Who doesn't enjoy walking barefoot through the grass on a warm summer day? I am thankful for the land of my birth and I am thankful for the land in which I live. I am thankful for the diversity of culture found throughout the lands God has given us. I am thankful for the land and what is cultivated upon it.

Day 153 Creation

At my cousin's wedding I heard the song "Sunrise, Sunset" for the first time. The song talks about how quickly the days have passed for the parents of the bride and groom. But really, it talks about how quickly the days seem to pass for all of us. I truly enjoy watching the sun rise and set. It is a miraculous masterpiece. Each day is different from the day before. Each sunrise and sunset, like each day, has different colors and hues, different nuances which make them unique and special. As we enjoy the sunrise or sunset today, let us stop and be thankful for the day we are living and everything that is special about it.

Day 154 Creation

Have you ever been to an aquarium or aviary? Or even better, a coral reef or scuba-diving expedition? Have you taken time to notice all the different species and array of fish and birds? There are so many! A student of mine believes there are still some lands and some species of animals, fish, and birds that have not yet been seen or discovered by man. I do not know about that, but I do know that God never ran out of ideas. Everything He created is unique and different and serves a unique and different purpose in its life. I am thankful for the many different kinds of birds and fish God created. I am also thankful that these remind us of just how unique and special we each are to God.

Day 155 Creation

I am thankful that God created people and animals. I am thankful for puppies. I am thankful for farm animals and zoo animals. I am thankful for pets, and I am thankful for meats. I am thankful that God has created people with a living soul to spend eternity in Heaven with Him some day.* I am thankful for babies and children. I am thankful for my friends and for older people to remind us of the right paths. I am thankful for the elderly and the handicapped who show us perseverance and the indomitable spirit, and give us opportunities to show Christ-likeness. I am thankful that God created people and animals.

please see epilogue for more information regarding this decision

Day 156 Creation

I am thankful for a time of rest: a time for reading, writing, or just being entertained with a good movie; a time for a nap, or just lounging on the couch. It is nice sometimes to be able to just relax and do nothing. A time to come away from everything and everyone else. Mrs. Evans, one of my college teachers, used to say that sometimes the most spiritual thing we could do is to take a nap. Even the Lord rested on the seventh day. I am glad for the times of rest and relaxation I enjoy.

Day 157

I am thankful for Saturday excursions to Little Rock. We did not have an awfully lot of them, but they usually consisted of a trip to Mardel's (the large teacher store), a clothing store if there were a good sale, a restaurant, and a TCBY or Coldstone's. These were nice, fun, little get-aways to experience once in a great while.

Day 158

I am thankful for Junior Church. I am especially thankful for Kindergarten Junior Church. I taught this class while living in Toledo and also in Arkansas. From my second Sunday here and for the next nine years, every Sunday found me with the primaries. I loved it. I started with the Creation story on promotion Sunday and taught through the Rapture each year. Little children love to worship and "love on" Jesus. It strengthened my walk with the Lord to be with the children who were excited to spend time in church learning about God.

Day 159

Arkansas is a very agricultural state. Rice and poultry are among our staple products. I enjoy fresh fruits and vegetables. Farm-fresh eggs just seem to taste better. I love the smell of hay and fresh cut grass. I am thankful for those whose life is spent growing and cultivating these good foods for the rest of us to eat and enjoy. I am truly grateful for farmers.

Day 160

I am also thankful for those who deliver foods and other goods to the markets for our convenience. We do not often enough stop and think about the life of a truck driver. He is away from his family several nights a week. He drives early and late to try to avoid rush-hour traffic. He has to be alert and conscious of the drivers around him. Above all else, he must be safety conscious. I am thankful for truck drivers.

Day 161 Graduation

I am grateful that this June I was able to attend my nephew's high school graduation ceremony. I am proud of both my niece and nephew and hope to return in a few years to also attend my niece's graduation. I acknowledge with him what an exciting though brief moment in life this touchstone can be. I celebrate with him the decisions he will make now that will guide and shape the whole of his adult life. I am thankful that his school had a formal ceremony and recognized those deserving of recognition. I am thankful that I have a niece and nephew of whom I can be proud.

Day 162

I love downtown Hot Springs! I am especially grateful to the shop owners here. My brother came to visit me here once. We went in to a souvenir shop downtown to get something for my niece and nephew. The owner talked to us for several minutes as he rang up our purchase. As we were leaving, my brother asked me why I had not introduced him to my friend. "My friend? Oh, the guy in the souvenir shop? I have never met him before." I am thankful for downtown Hot Springs and the wonderful people who work at keeping it special.

Day 163

One of my favorite downtown stores is The Toy Chest. They have a train table and other new toys out on the floor for the enjoyment of the patrons. I suppose this is probably my favorite because I have always enjoyed toy-boxes. My Grandmother's sister, Aunt Inez, had a box of toys comprised mostly of what her grandchildren had inadvertently left at her house on various occasions. When I was a child I would love to see what adventures I could have with the "leftover" toys. It always had a few blocks and Legos. It usually had some cowboys and soldiers and a few animals. Sometimes it had playing pieces from a board game. My brother and I could play for hours with those toy-box toys. I am thankful for the adventure and exploration that awaits inside the toy-box.

Day 164

I have previously mentioned many types of medical professionals, but I would also like to express my gratitude for their receptionists and office personnel. From the one who takes the call for the appointment, to the one who makes sure the chart matches the patient, to the one who calls the pharmacist and the insurance company: I am truly thankful for those who keep the records straight and keep the office running efficiently.

Day 165

I am thankful for those who serve our communities in professions that require their presence on Sundays. I will begin with policemen. I am grateful for patrol cars whose very presence keeps most of us from speeding. I am grateful for the officer who responds to the 911 call not knowing what might be in store. I am grateful for those who command authority at the scene of an accident when those involved may be overly emotional. I am thankful for those who have trained and prepared to be able to put on the uniform of a policeman.

Day 166

While living in Arkansas I have truly appreciated Riffle's Garage. It is run by a deacon of the church for which I came to teach. He is honest in his assessment of the damage and tries to completely repair my vehicle for as little money as possible. He will be giving it a thorough check before my move to Mexico. I am grateful for honest and trustworthy mechanics.

Day 167

I am thankful for those who clean our places of employment, learning, and worship. I think our society tends to look down on janitors. However, any honest and helpful work that is done to the best of our ability is glorifying to the Lord. I had a job once cleaning an office building from 6:30 am to 2:30 pm. It was hard work. In the last few weeks before my big move from Arkansas my student base slowly dwindled which caused me to take a job cleaning vacation rentals. Maybe these two experiences have helped me to appreciate janitors even more.

Day 168

The outside of our places of employment, learning, and worship also take much work to keep looking attractive and sharp. I appreciate young men who mow lawns for extra money and I appreciate professional landscapers. Arkansas is known as "The Natural State" and it is a very beautiful state. I am grateful for those who do their part to keep it that way.

Day 169

I am thankful for electricians. I am glad that I only need to flip a switch or push a button and the lights come on, the washer and dryer start, or my computer works. Electricity can be a dangerous entity. I am thankful for those who study its many facets and components and make it safe and convenient for us to use our electrical appliances.

Day 170

My job my senior year of college was cleaning dormitory restrooms. This meant I acquired at least a minimal knowledge of plumbing skills. I learned how to clean hair from the drain, unclog toilets, and snake a sink and toilet. Most of all, I learned that anything to do with bathrooms was nasty business. For these and many, many other reasons, I am truly grateful for professional plumbers.

Day 171

I am thankful for exterminators. Enough said.

Day 172

Like policemen, firemen also work on Sundays. I am grateful for volunteer firemen who train and prepare and show up to help when the need arises. I am grateful for full-time firemen who spend days away from their families so that they can always be ready when the siren sounds. I am thankful for the safety and protection we enjoy because of the men and women who wear the uniform of a fireman.

Day 173

It is official! Summer has begun! Longer days and shorter nights, warmer weather and more sunshine; I have always loved summer. As a kid it meant later bedtime and more outdoor time. As a young adult in college it meant trimming back the schedule to only work and no classes. As a teacher it brought a little more free time. Though with different stages of life it has held slightly different nuances, summer has always found me with great anticipation and expectation. I am thankful for the season that is summer.

Day 174

I am also grateful for the season of life that is summer. I am thankful for the many people and experiences that have formed my youth. I ran fast. I worked hard. I played hard. I loved much. I laughed a lot. And when I needed to cry I was seldom alone. I caught a few and I lost a few, but I chased my dreams. I truly lived in my youth and for that I am grateful.

Day 175

I am grateful for the cheerful cashier: the one who asks how you are and waits for an answer. The cashier who genuinely smiles and wishes you a pleasant day. The cashier who actually helps you with your purchase; who is not too busy to double check the price of the grapes; the one who actually believes that the customers are the reason she has a job. I am thankful for friendly cashiers.

Day 176

I am grateful for the road-trips which are a part of our summers. I have mentioned the destinations of a few by name, but today, I am just thankful for the journey: the talks in the car, the license plate and A-B-C games, the late night swims at the hotel, the trip itself. Whether with family or friends, or both, I am thankful for the joy of the journey as well as the excitement of the destination.

Day 177

While I was living in Arkansas, one of my friends since childhood drove down from Kentucky to get me and we enjoyed a memorable road trip. We saw "The Passion Play" in Eureka Springs, and then left for a tour of the state of Missouri. We went to the "Precious Moments Museum." We saw Laura Ingalls Wilder's home and Daniel Boone's homestead. We enjoyed Hannibal, Missouri, which is the setting for Tom Sawyer and Huckleberry Finn. We crossed the river to Springfield, Illinois, and saw Lincoln's law offices and the home where he raised his children. Our trip culminated with a visit to the Gateway to the West, the Arch in Saint Louis. We had a great time and a most enjoyable road trip.

Day 178

Though we had known each other since grade school, my friend and I found out on that road trip that we knew very little of the events that shaped our individual adulthood. Since we had last spent any amount of quality time together I had lost my mother. We had each experienced changed occupations and life directions. We were the same little girls that had played jump rope and tag, yet we had grown into very different and complex individuals. I am thankful for at least one friend who remembers with me my carefree self, full of dreams and hopes and expectations; at least one friend who can remind me of what once was and still should be truly important to me.

Day 179

Sunday drives. Family dinners. Afternoons at the park. Dinner on the grounds. Special singing groups. These are but a few of the many reasons I enjoy and am thankful for summer Sundays.

Day 180

I am thankful for Summer Camp. For several summers in Arkansas I served as a counsellor for Junior Camp at Triple S Christian Ranch. As a teenager, I attended teen camp at Mountain View Baptist Camp. I loved it as a young person and as a counselor. It is good for us to "unplug" from our daily distractions and focus only on our walk with the Lord for five whole days. I am thankful for the sports and games and contests. I am thankful for the swimming time. But most of all, I am thankful for the preaching and devotional time. Many of the decisions I made at Summer Camp as a young person were used to mold and shape most of the decisions I have made as an adult. I am thankful for Summer Camp.

Day 181

I am thankful for fishing! I love to go out on a boat and enjoy the river or lake. I enjoy the anticipation of the nibble on the line. One of my Dad's uncles would always grill all the fish we could catch when we went to visit him. My cousins and I would stay on the pond all day trying to catch as many big ones as we could. I remember one summer the boys would not let my cousin Debbie and I go with them to their "secret spot." They left us our little cousin, Tom age 3, and took off. Debbie, Tom, and I went out in the row boat. Tom baited the hooks for us and Debbie did most of the cleaning. The three of us caught twice as many fish as the five boys! I am thankful for memorable fishing trips.

July

Day 182

Is there anything man made that is more spectacular than fireworks? I love to sit out in lawn chairs or in the back of a pick-up and watch a fireworks display. It is always fun to bring some snacks and sit outside on a blanket and enjoy the show. One Independence Day the Perrymans took the boat out and we all watched the fireworks from the lake. All the colors, the noise, and the truly wonderful spectacles that are choreographed to patriotic music lend to the excitement. I am thankful for fireworks displays.

Day 183

I love patriotic decorations! Red, white, and blue streamers; Uncle Sam; flags; military themes – these all invoke a sense of pride for my country. I enjoyed these decorations on Central Avenue in Hot Springs and am sure other Main Streets, USA had similar displays. I enjoyed seeing them in stores and backyard barbeques. I am thankful for those who take the time to set the theme for patriotic celebrations such as The Fourth of July.

Day 184 Independence Day

The school I taught for in Arkansas celebrated "Heritage Day" every year around Thanksgiving time. I loved this day because the students would all choose someone in American History who had been instrumental in gaining or preserving our freedoms, dress in period costume for, and give a speech about, their patriot. In First Grade there were generally several George and Martha Washingtons, Betsy Ross', and Squantos and Pocahontas'. At the end, we would enjoy a re-creation of the First Thanksgiving. I am thankful for our founding fathers and all the sacrifices they made to give us the greatest nation on earth. I am thankful for those who still fight on the battlefield or in the capital to preserve the freedoms we will celebrate tomorrow.

Day 185 Independence Day

I am thankful for every person who stood against taxation without representation. I am thankful for every signature on our Declaration of Independence. I am thankful for John Hancock who signed large enough for King George to read without his spectacles. I am thankful for Samuel Adams and Samuel Chase. I am thankful for Benjamin Franklin and Samuel Bartlett. I am thankful for the well-known and the little-known. Each risked all and many lost all. Any amount of prosperity that we enjoy and often take for granted is only because of these men (and their wives) who valued freedom and independence above land or wealth. I would that we should be able to find such men again in our nation. Let us each be grateful for those who paved the way before us that we might have and enjoy the United States of America!

Day 186

In a time when many churches have stopped observing Sunday night worship service I would like to offer a word of encouragement to those who have not. I am thankful for Sunday night family church services. Only the youngest of parishioners are dispelled to the nursery. Young children and teenagers worship with their parents. The pastor offers words of admonishment or inspiration to the rest of us, many of whom were teaching classes ourselves in the morning, focusing on the special we were singing for the choir, or perhaps concentrating on visitors we had invited and making them feel welcome. There is just something special about Sunday night church; and I, for one, am thankful for it.

Day 187

Since my childhood I have enjoyed winding down from the problems of the day by watching some program in which all the problems of the world are solved in no more than sixty, and sometimes as little as thirty, minutes. It is unrealistic, I know. The situations are bigger than life and the solutions usually take a *MacGyver* approach. It somehow helps me to have a more realistic view concerning my own problems when Jan Brady's prom date is late or Beaver gets stuck in the coffee cup billboard. Andy always rescues Barney and the *Beverly Hillbillies* are hilarious. I am thankful for clean, humorous television shows that help me "unwind" from the pressures of life.

Day 188

I remember having a red *Radio Flyer* wagon as a youngster. My brother and I had so much fun with it. We would push each other down hills in it or race up and down the sidewalk in front of our house. When I was eleven or twelve, my friend across the street and I used that wagon in our leaf-raking business. I am not sure what became of that wagon, but I sure know that our enjoyment of it far exceeded whatever my parents paid for it. I am thankful for little red wagons and the innocent fun of long summer days.

Day 189

Also along the theme of the innocent fun of long summer days, I must also mention my bicycles. I have a few memories of a yellow tricycle as a toddler. My first two-wheeler was red with a white seat. I thought I was flying it went so fast! As I grew taller, I had others, usually passed down from my cousins since they only lasted one or two summers by size. All of us neighborhood kids would ride together to the local schoolyard to play on the swings or "pick-up" basketball or baseball. Sometimes we had races down the hill or around the block. I am thankful for bicycles and the fond memories made possible with my childhood friends.

Day 190

In my childhood summers there was never a greater day than when the grown-ups turned the sprinklers on! Oh how we kids loved to run through the sprinklers! And if more than one household on the same side of the street ran them on the same day it was like a marathon! We certainly loved the refreshing feel of the cool water splashing all over us. Like most neighborhoods, there was one older couple who did not allow the children on their lawn; but, we also had an older couple in our neighborhood who would turn their sprinkler on and come outside with cookies and lemonade just to enjoy watching us enjoy ourselves. I am thankful for the refreshing feeling of running through sprinklers in the yard. I am also thankful for refreshing and understanding older people who take time to enjoy the children around them.

Day 191

Who could possibly forget their first trip to the circus? The excitement of all the animals, the funny and entertaining clowns, the precision of the trapeze artist, the brave and courageous lion-tamer – all build on the excitement that is a trip to the circus! Each of our senses are inundated. So much to see and hear all at once! The smells of the animals mingle with the fragrance of cotton candy and hot dogs! From the audience it can seem as if everything is happening all at once with no rhyme or reason. In actuality, though, the circus is precisely timed with each act following its predecessor in accordance with the script they have practiced. Yes, I am thankful for the circus and its performers. But I am more thankful that when my life seems like a circus, I can know that each act is following its predecessor in accordance with the script the Lord has allowed for my life.

Day 192

I am thankful for softball. I played on a youth / adult league every summer from age thirteen through my college summers. After a few seasons in right field I graduated to first baseman. The shortstop and I played and practiced together for so long that I could catch her throws with my eyes closed. I also played intramural spring softball at the small college I attended. One summer in Arkansas I coached the Knucklers. My team in the youth / adult league won the league championship six years in a row and the regional division two of those seasons. My college intramural team endured four straight losing seasons. The Knucklers finished 2-14, with the top team in that league enjoying no-hitters against us in all but one game. The night Allison made it to first base against the maroon team, even the opposing parents were cheering. I am grateful that in softball, as in life, the great goal is in playing better in this game than the last one. The enjoyment of softball is in playing the game. Of course, it is more fun to win than to lose, but I am so thankful that I learned as a very young person that it is not about whether you win or lose, but rather it truly is all about how you played the game.

Day 193

Every church has one. Every Sunday School student knows who he is and where to find him. Even some of the adults seek him out each service. Of whom am I speaking? The candy man of course. He always has Jolly Ranchers or peppermints and sometimes Tootsie Rolls. These candies mysteriously appear before service or during handshaking time. One of my friend's dads always hid a Jolly Rancher between his fingers so you didn't realize you were getting a candy until after you shook his hand. I am grateful for those senior saints who remember how much fun it was to receive a treat for no reason. I am thankful for the candy man at church.

Day 194

At an office where I worked part-time one of my co-workers commented at lunch one day that I had leftovers for lunch more than anyone else in the building. She asked how I managed to have so many leftovers while asserting that I never cooked. "Well," I responded, "it is because I have so many friends who cook so well!" It was true: my neighbors saved me leftovers; my boss brought me leftovers; some of the parents of my students would bring me leftovers from Sunday dinner. Lots of friends shared lots of leftovers! I am thankful for leftovers and good friends who are willing to share them.

Day 195

I am thankful for the *Museum of Science and Industry* in Hot Springs. I am thankful for how much fun can be incorporated into learning. I have taken at least one group of students there every year I have lived in Hot Springs and each time I see something new. Usually the students would return with many questions which led into expanded reading time. Even after Siri, we still liked to read and look at pictures about the new exhibit. I think the toilet redesigned into a water fountain is a little over the top, but that is where every student wants his picture taken!

Day 196

The *Garland County Public Library* is another place that successfully incorporates fun into learning experiences. The children's department staff works hard at bringing in educational exhibits, especially in the summer. They have had cow-milking exhibits, snake-handlers, spoon players, living storybooks ... I could go on and on. Besides their knowledgeable staff and wide variety of reading, viewing, and listening selections, the library has many planned activities designed for family enjoyment. I am thankful for my local library.

Day 197

I am thankful for the *Hot Springs Parks and Recreation Systems.* We have so many trails and lakes. We have campgrounds and playgrounds. I especially like the giant fort at Cedar Glades Park. I have hiked to the top of West Mountain at least once per year I have lived here. One time, it was so hot that I nearly passed out, but I made it to the top! And, of course, I have to mention swimming in the creek after the hike! Entergy Park has the most natural variety. Family Park has the most playground equipment. DeSoto (Tank) Park is best for the little ones and has the easiest walking path. Linden Park has gymnastics equipment. I encourage you to get to know the parks system in your area and join me in being grateful for it.

Day 198

I am more thankful than I should be for the Shaved Ice stand on Albert Pike! The first time I went I was expecting a snow cone, which I really didn't care for as a child. Snow cones are basically Kool-Aid with way too much ice. But, the Shaved Ice stand does not sell snow cones: there is a unique and distinctive difference. I cannot quite explain it, but if you have experienced the difference you do not need it to be explained. I have not tasted these anywhere else in the United States, but I am very grateful that I have savored the flavors here in Hot Springs.

Day 199

Fresh blackberries! The mountain on which I have lived for ten of my fifteen years in Arkansas is abundant with fresh blackberries – yours for the picking! Of course, you must be mindful of snakes and ticks and wear gloves to protect your hands from the thorns; picking season is May and June, right at the beginning of the unbearable heat – but, oh my, is it ever worth it! I like to eat them as I am picking; I love the jam and the cobblers that my friends made when I brought them the berries. I am thankful for the abundance of fresh blackberries!

Day 200

Every church has one of these also. In my church, it is usually me; though occasionally in a larger congregation I am not alone. The entire congregation is in unison; each parishioner claiming his part resulting in the sound of a large melodious choir. Then the person of whom I am speaking today can be heard. Maybe a little low on the tenor, or maybe too squeaky when others ring true on the high ending note; but nonetheless heard above the beauty of the harmony, that one (or more) worshiper(s) who misses the note. I am thankful for every person who truly sings from the heart to the Lord. I am thankful for that person who is at least a little off-key but sings aloud to Jesus anyway. And, as that person, I am even more thankful for those who accept it, and by now should expect it; yet go on with the service as if the hymn were meant to be sung in that fashion.

Day 201

I am grateful to and for everyone who has been so encouraging regarding my move to Mexico. I am especially thankful for my Pastor and his wife who made the long drive with me (and then back again). I am thankful for those who have given financially to enable me to be here. I am thankful to the wonderful people here who have welcomed me and made me feel already at home. I am thankful for the peace that overwhelms my heart knowing that I am exactly where God wants me to be for this chapter of my life.

Day 202

I am thankful for little everyday things that make us feel better or more comfortable. Things like lotion or back-scratchers; things like aspirin or eye-drops; sure, we could definitely live without them, but our lives are so much easier with them. In this same way, I am thankful for smiles from strangers, waves from neighbors, or the times the driver in the next lane lets you in just to be nice. Words of encouragement from those who are not as acquainted with our daily struggles as our close friends might be. Today, I am grateful for the little things and the small gestures of kindness that brighten our days.

Day 203

I am thankful for scissors and staplers and, most of the time, copiers. I am thankful for mail openers and envelope moisteners. The little tools that make our lives so much easier; sometimes without us even realizing it. Most of us have at least a home office if we do not work at an office. Paperclips, pencil sharpeners, hi-liters, and colored pens all serve to help us in our daily plans and tasks. I am also thankful for the tools that help us in the kitchen: can-openers, paring knives, graters, strainers, baggies. I am thankful for grillers, choppers, and blenders. These are just a few more little things that we use every day and tend to take for granted. I am thankful that these exist and that they are readily available for our use.

Day 204

One more "little assortment of things" that we often take for granted: hugs and kisses from the little boys and girls that pass through our lives. They are little for such a short time and the window in which they freely pass these out is small indeed. It is no secret that the summer I am writing this finds me garnering every kiss I can from the little boys that brought me to Mexico. I cherish every one that is offered and am definitely not above asking for a few.

Day 205

Here in Mexico, almost everything is available with lime or chili flavoring; and sometimes, both. I love lime and am growing accustomed to the chili. There is lime in the mayonnaise, and there is chili for the popcorn. I like lime or lemons in my water. One of my new favorites, "elote" is corn on the cob which you can roll in mayonnaise, chili, lime, and / or peppers. Similarly, God has many different "flavors" or types of personalities to help us along in our travels through life. I am thankful for my punctual friends; I am thankful for my not-so-punctual friends. I am thankful for my "on-top-of-it-all" friends; I am thankful for my laid back friends. I am thankful for my "everything-has-its-place" friends; I am thankful for my "I know it's here somewhere" friends. I am definitely thankful that every one of my friends is different from me.

Day 206

I did not realize until I moved to an extremely hot climate in which I could not partake of the natural water just how grateful I *am* for water. Water soothes the throat and satiates our thirst. Although both are necessary for survival, a person can live a lot longer without food than without water. Over and over in the Bible we see the Word of God likened to water for our soul. Water; cool, clear, water, freely flows for all who would partake. Though both are necessary for spiritual health, a person can live a lot longer without church than without the Bible. Too often, though, we wait until our soul is dry and parched before we realize just how much we daily need its refreshing.

Day 207

I was overwhelmed with gratitude at the tremendous send-off my church planned for me the Sunday before I left for Mexico. We had a special speaker who gave a charge for going and sending for everyone regarding the Gospel. We had dinner between services. I gave a brief personal testimony and gave a word regarding God's leading to go to Mexico and what I would be doing when I arrived. Every person in attendance gave me money for my journey. And, more importantly, every person in attendance promised to pray for me. I am thankful for supportive friends. I am grateful for every church member who cheers on the missionary while continuing to participate in the ministries on the homefront.

Day 208

I am grateful for vitamins and sources of vitamins like fruit juice and vegetables. The little boost to our immune system that fends off the germs and helps keep us healthy. I take calcium and Vitamin C regularly and others during allergy or cold season. I am thankful that these small adjustments to our diets can have such a large impact on our health.

Day 209

I am thankful that fresh fruits and vegetables in Mexico are so inexpensive. I can eat things that are so good and healthful for me less expensively than I could eat ravioli and ramen noodles in the states. I am also thankful that God made so many different flavors and varieties of fruits and vegetables.

Day 210

I am thankful for Mexican food! It is so flavorful! I am thankful for the chili, the lime, and the peppers! I enjoy the old standbys like tacos, quesadillas, and burritos; but I am also enjoying trying new things and new flavor combinations. Similarly, in life, I am thankful for the heritage and traditions we observe; but am also grateful for the opportunities to experience the innovative and new. I am grateful to learn from other cultures and ways of life.

Day 211

I am thankful for snacks! Snack break has always been a part of my school (and work) day. It seems snack time is a part of the culture here as dinner is usually fairly late. Sometimes fruit, sometimes crackers with cheese or peanut butter, sometimes chips: but always there is time for a refreshing snack! I am thankful that God has placed similar "refreshment stops" along each of our life-paths. Sometimes in our devotions, sometimes a note or phone call from a friend, sometimes a church service: but always there is available just what we need to make it through the next leg of our journey!

Day 212

I love the mountains! I loved Peaceful Valley Mountain in Arkansas and never tired of the view. I am thankful that the Lord led me to a place of such beautiful scenery. Every time I walk out my door and in every direction, my view is of the beautiful majestic mountains of the Sierra Madre. I enjoy seeing them and hope I never get used to it. It is like being surrounded by a constant reminder of God's strength and beauty. Like the mountains, He is always there and never changing. I am thankful for these visible reminders of His majestic greatness and for His constant watch care and protection.

August

Day 213

I am thankful for the preparations that have been made for my arrival in Mexico. I am thankful for my home, my office, and my classroom. I am thankful for the school parents and students who built shelves, painted walls, laid tiles, and cleaned up afterwards, all of which has directly benefitted me. In this same way, I am thankful that I can rest in the knowledge that God has always been working for my benefit. Every place He has sent me has been prepared especially for me. He has worked the tapestry in every situation of my life to prepare me for the places He has sent and will send me. "The preparation of the heart in man and the answer of the tongue is from the Lord."

Day 214

More than at any other time in my life, I am thankful for every person who gives to missions. I am able to actually watch American dollars being used on the foreign field to bring others to a knowledge of Christ and to help them grow and abound in their Christian lives. I am thankful to have been raised by parents who sacrificially gave to missions. I am thankful for a Youth Pastor who taught on Missions giving to his teenagers. I am grateful to have had Pastors who continually kept the missions program in front of the congregation. Today, I am thankful for every church member who will use the line on their giving envelopes marked "Missions."

Day 215 Fruit of the Spirit

"Charity suffereth long and is kind; ... charity never faileth; " I am grateful that even at times when terrorism, hatred, and racism seem to run rampant in our society, there is still charity. There are still those individuals who choose love and forgiveness over hatred and retaliation. Think of the horrors of the Holocaust outweighed by Corrie Ten Boom's genuine forgiveness of her Nazi abusers. But also think of the every-day people in our communities who choose to demonstrate love and forgiveness every day. Who runs the women's shelter in your community?; the soup kitchen or food pantry? Do you know a couple who chose to be subject to the scrutiny of Child Welfare Services in order to offer a home to a foster child? I am thankful for every person who chooses love and forgiveness today. "And now abideth faith, hope, charity, these three; but the greatest of these is charity."

Day 216 Fruit of the Spirit

"Rejoice in the Lord alway; and again, I say, 'rejoice!'" "In everything give thanks; for this is the will of God in Christ Jesus concerning you." These verses are sometimes misinterpreted: "Rejoice always." And, "*for* everything give thanks." I do not believe God commands us to be thankful *because* someone we love has cancer, or we totaled our car, or experienced any other adverse situation or circumstance. Correctly interpreted, we can always find something in which to rejoice; in every situation or circumstance we can find a cause for praise. Can the cancer be treated? Do you have a support system of friends and family to help you through this? Can you be a part of someone's support system? Did your family make it through the crash? And above all else, if we have the Lord, we never face these situations alone. These words are definitely much easier to write than to live. I know I can do better, but I am truly thankful for every situation the Lord has used in my life to bring me closer to Him. I am thankful for the true joy that can only be found in Him.

Day 217 Fruit of the Spirit

"He that dwelleth in the secret place of the most High shall abide under the shadow of the Almighty." I am thankful that I can experience true peace through Christ regardless of the turmoil in the world around me. There will not be peace on earth again while mankind is still occupying the thrones of the nations. Jesus offers peace to anyone and everyone who asks. I am grateful for the calm that I can choose when my world falls apart.

Day 218 Fruit of the Spirit

"Strengthened with all might ... unto all patience and longsuffering with joyfulness." I am grateful for every person who has been patient with me throughout the journey of my life. I have never met anyone more patient than my Mom. My teachers were for the most part extremely patient with me (there were a few I learned other things from). I have friends who have been very patient with my quirks and dogmatic responses to life's vague questions. I am most grateful that the Lord is extremely patient with me. "His mercies are new every morning." Today, I am thankful for patience, given and received.

Day 219 Fruit of the Spirit

"But the wisdom that is from above is ... peaceable, gentle, and easy to be intreated, full of mercy ..." God says true wisdom shows gentleness. When I think of gentleness in general, I think of the hands of my Mother. She was always gentle with me. I remember even as a young girl hoping to have hands like hers someday. I always thought they were beautiful; and so gentle. Even when she was talking to me during my teen years about something in my life that should change, my Mom held my hand or stroked my bangs from my eyes. I am grateful that, like my mother's, even God's reproofs in my life have been administered with gentleness.

Day 220 Fruit of the Spirit

"The earth is full of the goodness of the Lord." Everywhere we look we can see the goodness of the Lord. Always His goodness is evident in natural beauty. Sometimes we see His goodness in the lives of those around us. Often, we are capable of sharing His goodness with those around us. Sometimes His goodness must be intentionally sought. I am grateful that God's goodness toward me does not depend on my goodness toward Him or others. I am thankful that whether or not it is immediately obvious, God is always good.

Day 221 Fruit of the Spirit

In Hebrews 11 we are provided a list of faithful men and women who endured "fiery trials of affliction" then admonished in verse 38: "Of whom the world was not worthy." To be sure, this statement is true of every name listed; but there are still men and women today of whom the world is not worthy. I am thankful for Jim and Elizabeth Elliot: one who died for his faith, and his wife who returned to the savages who killed him to demonstrate Christ's forgiveness. I am thankful for men like John R. Rice and Jack Hyles who gave their entire lives in service to reach and teach others. I am thankful for the faith of our fathers and our mothers. "Faith of our fathers living still in spite of dungeon, fire, and sword. Oh, how our hearts beat high with joy whenever we hear that glorious word. ... Faith that will pardon and cleanse within."

Day 222 Fruit of the Spirit

"I had fainted unless I had believed to see the goodness of the Lord in the land of the living." Faith patiently waits for the Lord to work in His own time. It seems like our world just grows worse and worse. There is more hatred. There is more violence. There is more and more wickedness. But, God is always working on behalf of good and right. I am thankful for those who came before us who believed God and stood for righteousness sake. "May all who come behind us find us faithful; may the fire of our devotion light their way. May the footprints that we leave lead them to believe. Oh! May all who come behind us find us faithful."

Day 223 Fruit of the Spirit

"...shewing all meekness to all men." True meekness is realizing that all men are created equal. True meekness is truly believing that "the Lord looketh on the heart." We all have weaknesses, faults, and failures. I am not better than you because my weaknesses are different from your failures. We tend to look too much to the outward appearance, athletic ability, or financial stability. I am thankful that I am just as important in the eyes of the Lord as Esther or Ruth. I am thankful that He saved me the same way He saved the woman at the well. I am not less than the queen; I am not greater than the servant. I am thankful that my worth has been determined by how much it cost the Lord to redeem me and not on anything that I have done or been incapable of doing.

Day 224 Fruit of the Spirit

"He that is slow to anger is better than the mighty; and he that ruleth his spirit than he that taketh a city." It would appear that self-control is harder to achieve than the defeating an army in battle. I feel certain that those who have attempted to beat an addiction would agree. I am thankful that I have never personally been chained to a controlling addiction. I am thankful for several people whom I love that have through the Spirit of the Lord reclaimed that city of self-control and beaten a harmful addiction.

Day 225

I am thankful for Youth Conference. For a few years the church I attended hosted a Youth Workers' Conference. These are a little different from camp mainly in that you stay in hotels or dorm rooms and have less outside activity. The emphasis is usually placed on the youth becoming the leaders of our next generation. I am thankful that there are a few teenagers who realize in their youth that there are some things more important than temporary pleasures; that keep the future and even eternity in view when deciding what to do with their lives. Some are called to the ministry during this week, but mostly for what I am grateful today are those teenagers who commit to rearing their children in the fear of the Lord, and to faithfully support their Pastor in whatever path their life's journey takes them. I am grateful for young people who decide to be better Christians and better citizens while they are young enough to keep from making decisions they may later regret.

Day 226

I remember oh so many summer evenings chasing and catching fireflies. We would put them in coke bottles or baby food jars just to watch their lights. We would see who could catch the most, which jar could shine the brightest. I remember doing this with both sets of cousins as well as in my own yard with neighborhood friends. I remember that it was more fun than TV! I remember that we did not have any video games yet. I am grateful to have learned how to make and have fun without needing someone or something to entertain me.

Day 227

Every August when I was growing up my family took a trip to the Florida Panhandle to visit my relatives on my Dad's side of the family. This was the time of his family reunion so we usually got to see all or almost all of our cousins. Sometime during those days that we stayed with my Great-Grandmother we would play Hide-&-Go-Seek in the dark in her huge yard filled with pine trees and bushes and all of our cars. There were a lot of places to hide. Sometimes we would play baseball in the cow pasture. One time, we all (around twenty of us from age four to age sixteen) walked a few miles down the road to the Chatahoochee River. We fished and waded. We were gone for hours and barely made it back just at dusk. Our parents were not in the least worried; I am not sure they realized we were gone. I am thankful for so many good memories of these times. I am thankful for the innocent fun times of childhood.

Day 228 The Whole Armor of God

I am thankful for Truth. I am thankful that in this ever-changing world there are still some absolutes; some immutable facts regarded as Truth. I am thankful for every person who will stand and teach Truth today. Some will teach Truth to their peers, some to young people, some to young couples, some to children, and some to mere babies in the nursery. I am thankful for every person who will seek to better themselves, their families, their relationships, their livelihoods by sitting and listening to the Truth today. I am thankful for every person who invested a part of their life in mine by teaching me and showing me the blessings of following after Truth.

Day 229 The Whole Armor of God

I am grateful for the "breastplate of righteousness." A breastplate is like a shield that you wear. Righteous behavior is an outward manifestation of a righteous heart. I am thankful for those people in my life who have proudly worn this breastplate whether they were praised or ridiculed. I am thankful for those times in my own life this breastplate has saved me from trouble or heartache. As a young adult, I was visiting with some friends I had not seen since high school. We were reminiscing about the "good-old-days" when one of them brought up a classmate's sixteenth birthday party and how cool it was that someone's uncle had brought liquor to the celebration. I looked at them astonished, not remembering this at all. They sheepishly looked at each other, suddenly knowing why I did not remember that event. The classmates throwing the party went to great lengths to ensure that a few other classmates and myself did not know of this party because they knew we would not participate and were afraid we would tell their parents. Our "breastplate of righteousness" had saved us from something that surely would have hurt our parents besides whatever other consequences may have ensued.

Day 230 The Whole Armor of God

I am thankful for the Gospel of Peace. This is the peace that passes all understanding. Not the absence of war; but peace in the midst of war and strife. Not necessarily the absence of hate toward me; but the absence of hate from within me. The feet of my heart, though not always shod with the preparation of this peace, *could* be always shod with the preparation of this peace. I am thankful that we can choose the Gospel of Peace. We do not have to live topsy-turvy lives in the midst of this topsy-turvy world.

Day 231 The Whole Armor of God

"Above all, taking the shield of faith . . . " Faith that God's plan is not just better than our plan, but that God's plan is always the best plan, is our shield from the "fiery darts of the wicked." Not faith that God will make a way, but faith that He has already provided a way. God has already met and fulfilled all of our needs. It takes great faith and sometimes courage to patiently wait for God to reveal His answer in His time. It is always easier to read or say these thoughts than to live by them. When you are the one on the chemotherapy couch; when you are the one whose company filed bankruptcy months before your retirement; when you are the one whose spouse has died or left you after fifteen or twenty years; when you are the one betrayed by your close friend: it is much harder to live by faith then. I am thankful that God has always been faithful and true to His promise; whether or not my faith was sufficient to wait for His answer, He has always worked for my good.

Day 232 The Whole Armor of God

I am grateful for the assurance of my salvation. I am grateful that my hope rests in the price Jesus paid for me on Calvary. I am thankful that my eternal hope does not rest in anything that I can do or feel. I am thankful that God has provided me with this helmet of salvation that can cause doubts and fears about the future to cease.

please see epilogue for more information regarding this decision

Day 233 The Whole Armor of God

I am thankful for "the Sword of the Spirit, which is the Word of God." In a separate entry I mention being thankful for the actual Bible, my copy of the Word of God. Here, I want to be a little more specific. I am thankful that for every question, problem, dilemma, or trial God has provided me with an answer in His Word. I am thankful for every promise in the Book. I am thankful for every blessing in the Book. I am thankful for the Word of God and the words of God. I am thankful for the stories in the Bible that clearly teach the outcomes of different ways of life. I am thankful that God's Word is clear and easy to understand. I am thankful for the Word of God.

Day 234 The Whole Armor of God

I am thankful for prayer. In the passage from which I have chosen topics this week it reads: "Praying always with all prayer . . . and perseverance . . . " I am thankful that I can turn to God in prayer in every circumstance. I am thankful that I can trust Him no matter how bleak the outcome may seem. I am thankful that He is never too busy. I am thankful that He is never impatient. I am thankful that He is always listening. I am thankful that I can pray and I am thankful for those who pray for me.

Day 235

I am thankful for the Bible. I am thankful for those men whom God used to pen it. I am thankful for those men whom God used to translate it. I am thankful for those who risked their lives so that God's Word might be preserved "to all generations." I am thankful for those who labor to translate it now for tribes who have yet to learn of Jesus and His love. I am thankful for my bi-lingual Bible which has been an invaluable tool to me while I strive to learn and master a second language.

Day 236

I am thankful for the first day of school each year. Ours here will be this week; no doubt some will be today; and further North, some will be after Labor Day. This day is a fresh new beginning. Everyone has a 100% A+ on the first day, for no one has missed any assignments or failed any tests. Eager faces sit before me anticipating the facts and skills awaiting them for this term. The younger the student, the more he wants to learn; the more he wants to conquer. Oh that I would nurture that desire within myself to learn and conquer some new thing today.

Day 237

I am thankful that in life, every day can be a day like the first day of school. Every day we can start fresh and eager. We can choose not to dwell on past failures or bad decisions. We can make the very best of all that is held within the twenty-four hours of this day. We can choose to be at peace with the Lord and ourselves regardless of what war may be raging in the world around us. I am thankful that "His mercies are new every morning." I am grateful for new days and new beginnings.

Day 238

There is so much in our lives that we are unable to comprehend. Even we math teachers must admit that some things are just beyond the human realm of understanding. We accept the law of gravity; but do we really know how or why it works? We believe the moon reflects the light of the sun; but do we truly understand how that works? We see the waves return to the shore; but why do they do that? I am grateful that God has placed some things in our world that are definitely beyond us. No matter how much time we devote to understanding it, it cannot be completely understood.

Day 239

George Washington Carver was pondering some of the mysteries of the universe and asked God to help him understand them and use the solutions to better mankind. His biography states that this wonderment led him to God's reply to his heart: "Let's start with the peanut." George Washington Carver then dedicated his life to learning everything he possibly could about the peanut. Hundreds of uses were discovered, many of which led other scientists to study other plants. I am grateful for the many things he discovered and invented, especially peanut butter! I am grateful for people who attempt to do great things while trying to change the world. Even if it seems like they are accomplishing little, only the Lord knows how many worlds will be changed.

Day 240

I am thankful for the logical progression of algebraic facts and geometric proofs. I am grateful that some things can be figured out and understood. I am thankful that at least for now, these subjects are still required in school. We use the logic we learned in Algebra every time we make a decision. From decisions as seemingly innocuous as which shoes to wear to life-changing decisions such as which college to attend, which job offer to take, or whom to marry. I am thankful for logic and the ability to use it. I am also thankful for the leading of the Lord and that I do not have to solely rely on what I am able to figure out.

Day 241

I am also thankful for "higher math" such as trigonometry and calculus that show us everything in life is relevant to every other thing in life. Think of terms like negative and positive, parallel and perpendicular, sine and tangent, similar and congruent. These are all mathematical terms that relate to our everyday lives. We speak of our life paths taking a curve or dip. If you can remember all the way back to graphing lines and curves then you know it will eventually even out. The highs and lows are congruent. The harder our trials, the greater the blessings to follow. Even if some of the mathematical terms of this entry taxed our brains a little, we can all be grateful that God is the great designer of our lives and nothing makes it on the graph without His approval.

Day 242

I am thankful for Scripture songs. When Bible verses are put to music, they are easier to memorize and harder to forget. I am thankful for the tapes and CD's that are available for aids in teaching these to children. I am thankful for the CD of Scripture songs in the Spanish language that was given to me to help me learn some Bible in my new language before moving.

Day 243

Do you remember having a towel tied around your neck and pretending to be Superman (or Supergirl)? Do you remember pretending that you could fly; or playing Aquaman at the pool? I am thankful for creative, imaginative, larger-than-life superheroes! My favorite is Batman. Batman does not need x-ray vision or elastic skin. Batman does not have to become someone else like the Hulk. Batman merely hides the fact that he is really mild-mannered millionaire Bruce Wayne and uses his extra sarcastic wit and super-powerful brains to outsmart the bad guys. Yes, I am thankful for super heroes and the magical time of childhood when I believed in them. I am also thankful to be a member of a league more powerful than the Justice League and to know that in the end our ultimate nemesis will be forever defeated.

September

Day 244

Do you remember thinking that your new tennis shoes could make you run faster when you were in grade school? I wanted to race everybody in class just to prove how fast they made me run. Of course, I know it was not the shoes. If I would be willing to admit it, I knew even then that it wasn't really the shoes. In that same manner, it isn't really us doing the accomplishing of anything in our lives. I am thankful for all that the Lord allows me to do. I am thankful for all He accomplishes through me. And, I am thankful that it is really Him doing the accomplishing.

Day 245

I am thankful for the beauty of the English language. I am thankful for authors and poets who have made it jump to life with a cacophony of onomatopoeia; those selections that make us feel what the author must have felt at the time of the writing; the stories that enable us to remember our childhood innocence; the poems that invoke the emotions of our first love; the classics that enable us to leave our world and enter another if only for a brief period of time. I am thankful for literature; and I am thankful for a teacher who took the time to teach me to appreciate it.

Day 246

I am thankful for the experience of learning new languages. I am just getting a grasp on Spanish. I can at least understand and be understood in simple conversation. I am looking forward to the day I can truly appreciate the subtleties and nuances that distinguish differences between similar items and situations. In this same sense, is that not how we learned to pray? Whether we learned as a child or as a new Christian, at first our prayers were simple words of asking and thanking. God always understood and has always answered in our best interest. As we mature in our prayer life, we begin to understand His patience and so we are more apt to wait for His answer. We begin to understand His forgiveness, and so we are more apt to forgive than to judge others. The Bible says we will never be able to fully comprehend God; but I am grateful that we can understand and appreciate Him better today than we did yesterday.

Day 247

I am thankful for Friday night youth rallies or youth activities. When I was a teenager my youth pastor always had something planned for Friday nights. Once a month, we had city-wide rallies including a Bible quiz and of course, food. Once a year we had "Records Night" to record who could do the most push-ups, sit-ups, etc.; who could eat the most pancakes; who could drink a coke the fastest; who could answer the most Bible questions. As an adult, I helped chaperone a weekly activity for the teenagers who rode the church bus on Sundays. At both events there was always a devotion or a sermon challenging us to live what we believed. I am thankful for those who give a part of their weekends to help young people have good clean fun as an alternative to what the world offers for weekend activities.

Day 248

I am thankful for game apps like Words With Friends, Word Chums and Trivia Crack. Not only do games like that keep my mind sharp, they make it fun to interact and keep up with those who have similar tastes in relaxation. I am thankful for the good fun I have with good friends playing these apps; I am thankful for the friends I have met through the tournaments and friendly competitions. I am thankful that Words With Friends is now available in Spanish which makes studying for my new language a more exciting challenge.

Day 249

I am also thankful for songs that teach character traits: songs like "O-B-E-D-I-E-N-C-E" and "Responsibility, That's the Key!" I am thankful for all of Ron Hamilton's Patch series. I am thankful for the songs that are incorporated in school plays that teach life lessons. I am thankful for the children's choir teachers that help them learn the songs and the Scriptural principles that accompany them.

Day 250

I am also grateful for literal words with friends – especially when those words are shared over a cup of coffee. Words about everything and nothing at the same time. Words that may not change the world, but yet may brighten the world of the hearer. Words of sympathy and compassion; words of strength and encouragement; words of love and life; words of laughter and sorrow; words of kindness and friendship: for all of these words shared with friends I am truly grateful.

Day 251

I am grateful for the darkened lenses of my sunglasses. There is just enough tint to keep the rays of the sun from distorting my vision. I can drive more safely and walk more comfortably. My sunglasses work in a similar manner as the things of earth work toward the things of Heaven. "For now we see through a glass darkly, but then face to face." Christ is so bright and holy that we are unable to fully see or understand His goodness in our lives. He has given us many representations of Himself through earthly truths so that when we do see Him face to face we will immediately recognize Him as pure and good and holy. Someday we will understand that everything He has allowed in our lives has been for good. So, yes, I am grateful for my sunglasses as well as the many other things in my life that God uses to help me recognize and understand Him.

Day 252

As I sit at my laptop typing these entries, I can see my umbrella in the corner of my room. It sits there in its place for weeks, maybe months, with nothing to do but wait. I never pay it any attention unless it is actually raining. I have had periods of my life that made me feel a little like an umbrella. It seemed I was not serving any purpose; it seemed I was helping no one. But then, one day, God opened another piece of His plan to me and allowed me to see I was not being useless, but rather I was just being prepared for the day He would use me for His greater purpose. I am thankful for my umbrella. I am thankful that no period of waiting is wasted in God's perfect timing.

Day 253

I am thankful for the first-responders who will get up and go to work today just like the rest of us, yet knowing in the back of their minds that any day could be a repeat of the horrors we will pause to remember tomorrow. There are a select few men and women who choose an occupation in which they are consciously placing the safety of others above their own safety. I am thankful that fourteen years ago, they more than met the challenge of the terrorists. I am thankful for their continued courage and dedication.

Day 254

I am thankful for every American citizen who will fly the flag at half-mast today. I am thankful for every citizen who will recite the pledge of allegiance or sing "God Bless America." I am thankful for every citizen who remembers the shock and awe we all felt when our great nation was attacked on our own soil. I am thankful for every reminder we will receive to be grateful for the freedom we enjoy that has been paid for with the life of someone else. Last of all, I am thankful for each person who will pause today and say a prayer. Let us pause in prayer for our nation to return to its roots. And let us pause in prayer today for every family who still mourns the loss of their loved one on this date.

Day 255

I am thankful for evening walks. Growing up, several of us in the neighborhood would walk several blocks together, then retire to someone's porch and drink tea or Kool-Aid until the darkness or the mosquitoes bid us retreat indoors to our respective homes. In college I would walk around our on-campus lake. As an adult I have enjoyed these walks with friends in our neighborhoods, at the park, or at or near the church or school. Sometimes alone, sometimes with a young person who needed a listening ear, and sometimes with an older person or friend who provided a listening ear. On rare occasions, I have even enjoyed early morning walks. The exercise may be needed, but there are so many more benefits from quiet walks.

Day 256

You have had a late lunch and are not quite ready for supper; yet, you are not quite full. You are dressed up, but maybe not quite as much as you were this morning. You want this time with your family to last a little longer before heading home and spending the evening preparing for the next day's activities. I am thankful for the trip to the ice cream store after Sunday night church. Dairy Queen or Sonic or the local Tasty Freeze is always crowded and always worth the wait especially on a warm Sunday night after service.

Day 257

At the time I am writing this I had just given handwritten thank-you-notes to a few well-deserving friends. I suppose these notes are rare now since there are so many new ways of communicating our thoughts and even our gratitude. The recipients were as excited as if I had given them their favorite candy bar or a gift certificate to the ice cream store. That started me thinking along the lines of why do I not give these more often? All of us like for our efforts toward the happiness of others to be recognized. Everyone enjoys the acknowledgement that comes with this gratitude. The note itself cost less than twenty-five cents; even if I had mailed it, it would still cost under one dollar. So, basically, it cost me little more than the time it took to write it. I am grateful for such an inexpensive way to let others know that I notice and appreciate the things they do for me and the things that they are to me that make my life's journey more enjoyable.

Day 258

I am thankful for simple and easy crafts. I never did well in craft-time in elementary school. Maybe those skills are in the same hemisphere of my brain as my non-existent musical abilities. But a friend of mine has been sending me some simple paint-and-assemble crafts that even I can do with young children. They love it and I get to feel a little bit like a hero. I am thankful for the sense of accomplishment that accompanies completed projects, no matter how small. I am grateful for my friend who sends me these projects. I am glad the boys enjoy doing them. I am grateful for the foundations these simple crafts are laying that will later serve the boys when they start helping their dad with larger and longer lasting projects.

Day 259

While writing yesterday's entry, I was reminded of some of my failed elementary school projects. There was the coffee mug that my parents thought was an ashtray. There was some sort of craft involving color schemes made with yarn and paints that I threw away in frustration trying to explain. I once made a diorama of the first Thanksgiving that looked more like the War of 1812. But I digress; I want to tell you for what I am grateful from these experiences. I am thankful for teachers who understand that doing is a part of learning. While making these projects life lessons were implanted into my brain. God, the true potter, knows what He is making whether or not His masterpiece is discernible by others. God, the master painter, sees only the beauty in all of the colors He allows into our lives. God, the artful sculptor, always sees the whole picture including all of the details, and knows exactly where each piece will fit perfectly. I am thankful that even when I am frustrated and discouraged with my oh-so-many mistakes and failures that God can take all of the pieces and weave them into a beautiful and useful masterpiece.

Day 260

One such craft I will never forget is a macramé holder for hanging pots. Even when I had chosen what I thought was a beautiful rustic orange color yarn, my friends commented that it looked more like dirt or a rotten squash color. Undaunted, this was to be my one great accomplishment. I was no longer in elementary school; my junior-high project was going to be a Mother's day present my Mom would treasure for her lifetime! I carefully and painstakingly followed all of the directions. I tied every knot with love; I strung every bead with patience. In the end my intense labor earned a C+. I was devastated. How could I give my Mom a C+? But I did give it to her, assuring her that even though it hadn't turned out as beautifully as I had imagined it, I hoped she could use it. My Mom gushed with pride! That's just the color she would have chosen! Those knots were sturdy enough to hold even her large potted plants! And so, even though it appeared to be a hideous monstrosity to every other eye that beheld it, to my Mom it was a beautiful expression of love. That hideous monstrosity did become the Mother's Day present that my Mom would treasure for her lifetime. It was still hanging in her kitchen on the day she died, almost twenty years later. I am grateful that my Mom used the eyes of her heart much more than the eyes of her head. I am grateful that this is also the way the Lord sees our attempts to please Him. When we act from a heart to please Him, He sees only a beautiful expression of Love.

Day 261

I am grateful for times of pretend. I am thankful that I grew up in the era of "Sesame Street" and "Mr. Rogers' Neighborhood." I am thankful that I could be anything I wanted on any given day. A hat, or a certain color shirt and suddenly I was someone else. Our array of wooden blocks became all sorts of tools and weapons. I loved to play dolls or Barbies. I also loved to play cowboys and Indians with my little brother. Unlike we later discovered in the real world, the good guys always won in our world of make-believe. Ken and Barbie always lived happily ever after. I am thankful for the fun and memories attached to these days; but I am also thankful for the life-lessons I learned while pretending. I *could* be anything I wanted to be. I just had to be willing to put in more work than was required to change my hat or shirt. I *could* be someone that met the needs of others, if I would be willing to work outside of my job description. I am so grateful for the world of make-believe that has influenced my imagination and fostered my ability to believe in myself and others.

Day 262

I love a freshly sharpened pencil! I especially love a freshly sharpened pencil if I am working on Algebra or Geometry. I love the smell; I love the feel; I love the way the point glides across the paper. I have even written out many of these entries in a spiral notebook using freshly sharpened pencils. I am thankful for freshly sharpened pencils. Sometimes when life begins to seem dull or monotonous, we just need a fresh perspective to sharpen our focus. If we sharpen our attitudes, we may improve the way we fill in our days even if we cannot change what is written.

Day 263

Where is the nursery? Where is the ladies' room? Could you help me find a seat in the service? I am grateful for the ushers and greeters who answer these and many more questions every week. I am grateful for the quiet passing of the offering plate, the gauging and adjusting of the temperature, and many other things that I may not even know they are doing for the service. Their goal is to simply enhance the worship experience for the rest of us. I am thankful for those who serve when needed whether or not they are seen or publicly appreciated.

Day 264

Sometime today we will observe the official beginning of fall. Crisp breezes, falling leaves, autumn smells, beautiful arrays of colors: these all begin to inundate our senses. We drag our forgotten jackets and sweaters from the closet. We breathe more deeply. We walk more briskly. We seem to be able to think more clearly than we did in the heat of summer. We burn harvest-scented candles. By now, we have settled in to our school-year routines. I am thankful for the season of fall. I am thankful for the changing of the weather from hot to mild. I am thankful for the routine and ordinary that helps us to better appreciate the extraordinary.

Day 265

I believe as I am writing this, I am just beginning the autumn season of my life. I have begun to reap some of what I sowed during my spring and summer seasons. I am gleaning some blessings from my labors of teaching and investing in others. I often feel my senses inundated with memories. I feel myself in more of a hurry to accomplish some of my life goals. I see what should be my priorities more clearly than I did in my often selfish thoughts of my summer. I am thankful for my ordinary life that can be used by God to accomplish His extraordinary purposes.

Day 266

In the Lord's work, we are not always privileged to see results on this side of Heaven. I am very thankful for the blessings I am reaping now as a direct result of previously sown seeds of influence. There are two little boys who run and jump with excitement and hugs whenever they see their "Aunt Emy." (There are actually three little boys, but as of this writing, one of them cannot run, jump, or hug yet.) I am grateful for the opportunity to be a part of their lives and share in the love with which they are surrounded. I am grateful for every decision that has led to this season of harvest. I am grateful for every person who decided to invest a portion of their lives in the young people of the next generation. I am grateful for every minute I spent walking on Luna Pier or driving to the Perrysburg Ice Cream Store. Who could have even imagined the blessings that would be realized as a result of what seemed at the time mundane, every day occurrences? I am truly grateful that the Lord is allowing me to reap such wonderful benefits in my autumn harvest.

Day 267

One fall, a friend and I took some pre-teen girls to Tennessee to tour The Great Smoky Mountains. We had prayed that the trip would be fun while also educational. We explored Cade's Cove with a retired history teacher as our tour guide. The girls loved the Wonderworks Museum! We braved the giant Ferris wheel. We embarked on the Titanic where we each "became" a passenger for the fateful journey. The girls were given cards of sisters whose father was the only black man aboard. We learned not only of the Titanic, but also of unfair, yet accepted, racial policies of the day. Thankfully, all of our passengers survived. We also toured the re-making of an old town square. We spent some good quality time enjoying the pool also. As a bonus, I am thankful that my friend and I were deemed "cool adults" by the girls on that trip. I am thankful for the rich beauty of The Great Smoky Mountains. I am thankful for good friends with which to share this beauty.

Day 268

That trip reminded me of the time my parents took my brother and me to The World's Fair in Knoxville in 1982. We learned and experienced so much. I thought at the time that my parents just loved camping, but actually, we took a camper because we could not afford hotel rooms. We saw demonstrations of the newly developed technology now known as the mobile phone. Somewhere is a picture of us getting drenched on the "flume" ride. What I remember most about this trip, though, is that my brother and I had to agree to a truce – no arguing or even disagreeing for the entire trip. My Dad promised that if we broke the truce he would drive the camper home. We believed him. For seven days in a row once in 1982, not one person in my family said a cross word, no one raised his or her voice, no one argued about anything. We enjoyed each other and our trip to the World's Fair. I am thankful that at least once in my life I have experienced a World's Fair. I am also thankful that for at least one week during my teen years my family enjoyed me.

Day 269

I am thankful for jackets. Just a little warmth to pull over your selected outfit in case there is a breeze or a burst of air-conditioning. I like blazers and sweaters that complement your outfit but can be removed in case it gets too warm. I am thankful for friends in my life who have known me well enough to know when I need just that little touch of encouragement like the touch of warmth from a sweater or jacket.

Day 270

As the rights and freedoms once thought guaranteed by our Constitution are swiftly disappearing, I would like to express gratitude that we still enjoy the freedom to worship God in the way we feel He wants us to. I encourage each of us to exercise that right this week. I admonish each of us to be willing to fight to preserve this freedom as our forefathers were willing to fight to obtain it.

Day 271

Whether they are noticed or neglected; whether they are heeded or ignored, the lighthouse stands as a bastion of hope and safety and points to the way we each should take. I am thankful for those leaders in our communities and churches who stand and shine a light on the right paths; those individuals who consistently take the high road and live above the pettiness that too often defines our culture. They are like the beautiful lighthouses that adorn our seacoasts. I am thankful for lighthouses, both figuratively and literally.

Day 272

I am thankful for night lights and flash lights. When the path or your room is truly dark, and you are not sure what obstacles may have been left in your way, it is nice to have just enough light to see the next step. I have had such friends in my life also; maybe not lifelong friends, but good friends who helped me through a dark season. I am thankful for those people God has brought into my life at exactly the time I needed them with just that right amount of encouragement to help me take the next step.

Day 273

I am thankful for my bedside lamp: the lamp that I only turn on if I am reading or writing after dark alone in my room. This is the lamp that I only turn on when the other lights in the house are turned off. This is the lamp that I only use when I really need it. Likewise, I am thankful for those friends in my life that I know I can count on no matter whether others are with me or not. I am referring to the friend that I may not see or speak to every day, but whom I know I could call in the middle of the night and they would answer. This friend would talk me through my crisis. This friend would offer to come to me if I really needed them. I am also grateful to be likened to this bedside lamp for at least a few of my friends.

October

Day 274

I am thankful that I discovered a love and a penchant for writing while I was still young. Today, I would like to share with you "October Sunset" written during my freshman year of college:

October is such a beautiful time of year

The stately trees are all changing their leaves

Acorns fall

And pumpkins all

Grow and are picked and are carved

In go the sneakers; out come the boots

We dig out our socks and our sweaters

To go out and admire the beauty of nature

We rake the leaves and pile the kindling

I know not why but there seems to be

More hustling and bustling and hurrying

Here, there, and everywhere

All these things and places and all at once

But, however cold or cool

Nothing quite compares

To a sunrise in October

No matter how beautiful or fair

Unless perhaps at the end of the day

God's paintbrush exhibits

An equally beautiful sunset

Day 275

I am thankful for flannel. I love to wear an oversized flannel shirt over a t-shirt during the fall. I think this started with me wearing one of my Dad's shirts to a church hayride one time. It was so comfortable. It was just the right amount of warmth during the ride and yet not too much warmth around the bonfire. I know there are people who would rather dress more nicely than is possible while sporting a flannel shirt; but, I for one am for the comfort and convenience of flannel whenever remotely appropriate. I am thankful also for these types of people in my life. I am thankful for people with whom I can be completely myself and feel entirely comfortable around. I am thankful for those friends who have accepted me into their circles and with whom I can don my "flannel and cotton" and leave off my "dressed-up" public persona.

Day 276

Although I am very thankful for the changing season, I would like to take a moment on this day and express my gratitude that the Lord has placed me in an area of the world in which it is still warm. I am so grateful that it is not snowing at my house today. I am grateful that I will not have to shovel my drive or walkway this month. I am grateful that it is highly unlikely that I will need to shovel snow at all during the whole of the winter season. I am thankful to enjoy the cooler temperatures without the eminent threat of ice and snow.

Day 277

I am grateful for those ladies who voluntarily miss out on the service in a rotating schedule to watch over those parishioners too young to appreciate the service. Of course, I am referring to the nursery workers. Thank you for rocking the little ones or playing hide and seek. Thank you for feeding and changing your little charges while we are singing hymns and listening to our charge for the week. We should all be thankful for the nursery workers.

Day 278

I am thankful that the Lord has always had people in place in my life to challenge me out of mediocrity. I have had Pastors, teachers, and friends who have challenged me to reach in deeper, to reach out further, so that I could become more than I could realistically dream possible. I am thankful for those friends who have encouraged me to become my best self. Whether or not I have risen to the challenge, I am grateful that the Lord has always had someone in place to help me see myself as others see me and to help me keep my priorities in line with the truly important aspects of life.

Day 279

If we would take the time to think about it I believe we would all agree to be thankful for our everyday hygiene: toothpaste, deodorant, soap, shampoo, etc. I am also thankful for mints and gum as well as perfume and cologne that help make us more presentable in public settings. We indulge in these items for our own benefit as well as for the benefit of those around us. Along these same lines, we should view our prayer and Bible reading time. When we devote some time each day to the Lord and seek to cleanse our minds and renew our spirits we are more ready to face the challenges of the day and are more likely to be a blessing to those with whom we share our days.

Day 280

I am thankful for the lessons we can learn from the story of Adam and Eve. We can learn that Satan always devises a way to make sin seem desirable and pleasant. We can learn that Satan always attempts to mask the consequences of sin. We can learn how easy it is for us humans to fall for the charades of the serpent. We can learn to recognize Satan's most successful and thus most repeated lie: "Only one taste won't hurt you; just try it one time." I am thankful that we see God's plan for our redemption from the beginning of creation. And most importantly, we can learn that God always provides a means of forgiveness.

Day 281

I am thankful for the institution of the home. I am thankful for the choice of marriage. I am not married; but I am thankful for those who are. My parents were married; as was most of the parents of those of you reading this. I am thankful that my parents stayed married until my Mom went to Heaven. I am thankful that my father has remarried since, and found happiness again. I am thankful that two people can freely and deliberately choose to walk the steps of life together. These two people can make a home together. These two people can choose to have children and raise them according to their own spiritual, religious, and political beliefs. I am thankful for marriages and homes.

Day 282

I am thankful for the lessons we can learn from the story of Cain and Abel. We see that God has only one way and only one plan for us to come to Him and that His plan has nothing to do with the fruit of our own labors. We see that jealousy is but a step away from hatred. We see what Jesus Himself confirms for us in the Gospels: that hatred and murder stem from the same part of our heart. We see that God does indeed hold us responsible for the way we treat our brothers. We see God's vengeance and His mercy both in the same story.

Day 283

I am thankful for the relationships we can have with our brothers and sisters. I have one brother whom I love and respect. Though I did not really realize it at the time, my brother was my first friend. We had our share of arguments and selfishness when we were children. However, when we were in our teen years our priorities were jolted into place with my Mom's cancer diagnosis. Years later, as young adults when my Mom's cancer returned, we grew even closer. My brother understands me. I feel like he knows what I mean even if my words are insufficient. I am truly thankful for my little brother.

Day 284

I am thankful for the close relationships we can have with our brothers and sisters in Christ. Of course, we should love and pray for one another always; but some of my fellow worshippers have come to be regarded in the same sense as family. Our hearts have been knit together in a special fashion. I like to reference the words God used regarding David and Jonathan when I describe this kind of relationship: "he loved him as he loved his own soul." He loved him as himself; he loved him as his own family. I am thankful for those who have loved and accepted me like family. I am thankful for the opportunity to display this Christ-like love to others.

Day 285

I am thankful that none of us have to live in the past. I am thankful that even though some of our actions have long-lasting consequences we do not still have to continue on in the same pattern of living that caused them. I am thankful that those that love me do not bring up all of the stupid things I have done or said. I am grateful that my parents taught me not to bring up the failures in the pasts of others. Whatever it has become, it is what it is now. The present is where we live. The present is with what we should concern ourselves now.

Day 286

I am grateful to be living in the age of information. I am thankful for the six-o'clock news and news programs on FOX and CNN. I am glad that we have reports of nationwide and worldwide events at our fingertips. We can learn about almost anything we choose to with the click of a button. I am thankful for the reporters and the anchormen who bring us these newscasts and journalistic stories that help us grow into better well-informed citizens.

Day 287

I am thankful for children's storybooks. I loved them when I was the child being read to and I have grown to love them even more as the reader. I am thankful for authors like Getrude Crampton who painstakingly strove to convey a principle to live by while using settings, people and objects that would interest the child. My Mom did *all* the voices when she read "The Three Bears" and "The Three Little Pigs." I am also thinking of "Scuffy the Tugboat," "Tootle," "The Little Engine that Could," and many, many others. When I taught First Grade for oh-so-many school years I referenced characters from these stories almost as often as Bible characters when teaching and training desired behavior. I am thankful for these stories and I am thankful that my mother read them to me.

Day 288

I am grateful for two little boys who crawl into my lap and love to hear me read. I am thankful that they enjoy books and the pictures and stories within their pages. I am thankful for my Great Big Book of Bedtime Stories from my childhood that contains thirty-two all-time favorite children's tales. I pray that these boys will grow in their love for reading and learning. I am thankful to be a part of their formative years. I am glad I get to be one of their teachers.

Day 289

I am thankful for the story of Noah and the Ark. I am grateful that there was at least one man who believed God would do what He said He would do. I am thankful for the fact that God still delivers all who will believe. I am grateful that his family believed that Noah walked with God and endured the ridicule and rejection that came because of the path he chose to follow. I am thankful for the rainbow at the end of the story that symbolizes the keeping of God's promises. I am grateful that He has kept every promise He has ever made.

Day 290

I have previously expressed my gratitude for Jenny and her boys, but today I would like to express my thankfulness for the man who captured first her attention and then her heart. I am thankful that he has consistently worked at keeping both. I am thankful for his hard work and long hours and the sacrifices he makes to keep his family safe and comfortable. I am thankful that in a world that is swiftly declining in its respect for manhood that this man remains a strong example to his boys of hard work, faithfulness, dedication, and other character traits that are the building blocks of Christian manhood. I am grateful for his respect for and loyalty to his parents. I am grateful for his faithfulness in even the little, seemingly insignificant things of every day life. Jon, I am thankful for you, and for each plane on which our lives have intersected.

Day 291

I am thankful for "Sword Drills." We had these often in Sunday School and in the Christian school I attended growing up. It was great motivation for learning the Books of the Bible. I seldom won even a few points and don't ever remember winning the game. But it was a fun and encouraging way to impart the importance of knowing how to use the Bible. I am grateful for those who used childlike methods to impart knowledge and principles I have needed in every stage of life.

Day 292

I am thankful for the story of Joseph. Here is a man who stayed faithful to what He knew of God even after he had been twice betrayed by those he thought he could trust. Through his realization of the goodness and forgiveness of God, he was able to also forgive. I believe Joseph forgave his brothers long before the moment they stood before him. I believe he also forgave Potiphar and his wife. Although I cannot find this forgiveness recorded as plainly as that of his brothers, we do see a man wholly committed to trusting God and His plan. We see no bitterness in the life of Joseph. This lack of bitterness is what leads me to believe that Joseph lived a life of forgiveness. I am grateful for the story of Joseph because of the possibility it conveys for me to live a life of forgiveness free of bitterness and resentment.

Day 293

I am thankful for the story of Moses. Here is an ordinary boy born into an ordinary family, yet raised in the palace as a prince. The Bible tells us though that when "he was come to years" he chose to go back to ordinary. I know Moses was used to show the mighty power of God in many miraculous ways. However, the first miracle happened when the man in line to the throne of the greatest kingdom of the world at that time chose to be ordinary. I am thankful for the simplicity of this profound truth: God can work in extraordinary ways with those who choose to remain ordinary in the sight of the world.

Day 294

I am thankful for the story of Joshua. Here we learn of a young man who stayed faithful to God and the man of God throughout his youth and grew into a mighty warrior. Joshua led the armies of Israel to some of their greatest victories. I am thankful that God chose also to record some of his defeats and how this mighty warrior handled those as well. I am thankful that through the life of Joshua we can see the importance of fighting for your nation and her freedoms. I am thankful for the story of Joshua and I am thankful for the Christian men and women wearing a uniform of the armed forces of the United States of America.

Day 295

I am grateful for the story of Ruth. This young woman chose to follow what she believed to be the path God had chosen for her even if it meant she would never marry and have children of her own. I do not know much of Ruth's family in Moab, but I doubt that they were as poor as she and Naomi were when they returned to Naomi's homeland. It was more important to Ruth to identify with the Lord than to have or become anything else. I know that before the end of the story, Ruth does marry the wealthy kinsman Boaz and she does indeed have children of her own. But, just as we do not know our own stories, Ruth did not know the end of the story when she made her decision. I am thankful that I can rest in the fact that whatever God chooses for me will be better than any plans I can conceive or devise.

Day 296

There are probably more stories and applications from the life of David than any other Bible character apart from Jesus Himself. The stories of David reveal so much to us of the human experience. We see his entire life from a hopeful bright-eyed shepherd boy, to the youth throwing caution to the wind who faces and defeats the mighty giant. We see him as a loyal friend and a mighty warrior. We see him fall in love and we see him fall in adultery. We see him both as a foolish and indulgent parent with Absolom and as a wise and loving father with Solomon. We see him as a servant to Saul and watch expectantly as he becomes the king. In the Psalms we see battle cries as well as songs of comfort and peace. We see David's heart and all that is in it. We see him in times of revenge as well as in times of forgiveness. We see his hopes and we see his despair. I am thankful that God allowed us to see so much of the heart behind the actions of David. I am thankful for what I can see and learn of myself from the story of David. And, I am thankful that God judges the intents of my heart over the results of my actions.

Day 297

My favorite Bible story is the story of David and Jonathan. Two young men who develop a friendship in their youth and decide to remain loyal to each other regardless of the words or deeds of their families or other friends. We see two young men whose friendship endured even when one falls in love with the other's sister. A friendship that survives one of them being promised the throne that rightfully belongs to the other. A friendship that survives one of the men's fathers attempting to kill the other friend. We never see Jonathan being jealous that David will receive his throne. We never see David speak ill of his best friend's father even after a bounty is placed on David's life. We never once see recorded David doubting Jonathan's loyalty to him. I am thankful that this kind of friendship can still be attained. I am thankful for my friends who decided to remain loyal to me despite my faults and my failures. I am thankful for my friends who have been there for me, wherever "there" happened to be. I am even more grateful that I also have family members who can be counted in that group of friends.

Day 298

Today is the birthday of one of my "David and Jonathan" friends. As I am writing this entry she has just agreed to enter a testing period to try a new medicine in the ongoing war against cancer. When she told me she had decided to do this, two statements rang out to me over the din of the echoes of little or no hope offered by the doctors. The first was that she seemed to be much more concerned with her students adjusting to hearing her news than she was with her own adjustments. The second was that she was joining the trial without hoping to get better; she was agreeing to the clinical trial in hopes that her participation would serve to help others in years to come in their battle with this horrible disease. I am thankful for our enduring friendship. I am thankful that I am privileged to know a real hero.

Day 299

I am thankful for bags. I am glad I do not have to juggle everything I am trying to carry, or worse, have to make several trips from the car or up and down the steps. I am especially grateful for those bags that have pockets and sections for organizing what I need to carry. I am thankful also for what some would call "baggage." I am not happy that my previous relationships failed in the "always and forever" category. But I am thankful for what I learned about myself: both my aspirations and my limitations. I am thankful for what I learned about love: both its whimsical fantasies and its realistic ambitions. I am grateful that someone chose to love me and I am thankful that I chose to love. Therefore I am grateful for the baggage those choices have created.

Day 300

I am thankful for good old, down-home, country-style gospel music. The kind you can tap your foot to; the kind you can sing along with on a road trip. I especially enjoy the songs that talk about the stories from the Bible or the experiences of the songwriter growing up in church. I am thankful that an entire station of Pandora is dedicated to this genre. I love to sing the old ones and listen to the new ones. I understand that the Christian life is not about emotions and some of these selections may not be appropriate for a worship service. I enjoy the uplifting attitude I find myself in throughout the day when I have been playing these old stand-bys throughout the morning.

Day 301

I am thankful for coolers and thermoses. I am thankful these items come in a variety of sizes and can be used for taking things to school or the office or on large picnics. These handy contraptions keep hot things hot and cold things cold. They stabilize their contents. I know I sometimes need stabilizers in my life. Prayer and coffee are my daily stabilizers. Sometimes I need encouragement. Sometimes I need a reality check. Sometimes I just need to know that someone is on my side. I am thankful for the stabilizing elements of my life.

Day 302

I am thankful for notecards and notebooks, including the notebook app on my phone: a quick place to jot down new information or a good idea so as to not lose it. Occasionally the notebook app of my brain takes a note of what made a certain principle or concept finally click; or records a snapshot of a special moment in time. Sometimes these pages abruptly come to the forefront prompted by some similar happening; sometimes prompted by something as simple as a fragrance or a sound. Sometimes these pages bring sweet memories, and sometimes bittersweet. I am thankful for the little interruptions flashed across my mind of long ago, seemingly forgotten, memories. I am thankful for the whole of my experiences and for the person into which they have shaped me.

Day 303

Campfires, hayrides, roasted marshmallows, and s'mores: all these have been such an enjoyable part of my fall experiences since I was very young. I love the smell of the hay and the fun of laughter and singing while riding along at a friend or neighbor's farm property. Then just before dusk the gathering at the bonfire to roast hotdogs and marshmallows is sure to bring more laughter while drinking apple cider or hot chocolate. Talking, sharing secrets and stories; just enjoying being with our friends with no paperwork, pressures, or deadlines. I am thankful for the fall weather and these times to enjoy being outdoors together before winter arrives.

Day 304

When I was kid, I loved trick-or-treating! Everyone I knew participated in this practice. I am thankful that I grew up in the times before evil usurped the fun of dressing up like a princess, a cowboy, an animal, or even a monster; then going door-to-door asking for candy, *and actually getting it!* I remember having a blue and black cowgirl outfit that I loved so much I wanted to wear it again on Easter. I remember other costumes and masks. It was just a fun day. We kids always ate more candy than our parents wanted us to, and we would still have enough to take a piece or two a day in our lunchboxes at least until Thanksgiving. I am thankful that even as a Christian young person I could enjoy this time without politics or wickedness entering into it. I am thankful that my parents did not have to worry about drugs or needles being given to us. I am thankful that my non-Baptist friends and neighbors did not wonder if my family had suddenly abandoned our religion. I realize that there is so much stigmatism attached to so many things now that choosing whether or not to participate is not this simple. I am thankful to have grown up in an era where fun was recognized as fun and we could all just have a good time. I am grateful to have grown up in a simpler, much less complex era of America.

November

Day 305

The air is crisp and clean! There are beautiful autumn colors everywhere! Autumn even brings its own aromas! Everything looks and smells exciting! I am thankful for the season that is fall and today I am especially grateful for the Sundays that fall in this season. There is just something special about going to the House of the Lord on a beautiful autumn morning.

Day 306

I am thankful that I grew up in an era when the office of the President of the United States was still viewed as an office of leadership. I am thankful that when I was growing up, other nations had respect and not contempt for our President. I am thankful for those Presidents who first served in uniform before desiring to serve in the White House. I am thankful for the Presidents who attempted to stop communism and terrorism. I am especially thankful for those who succeeded in at least staving off these evils for another generation. Whether or not I agreed with their policies, I am thankful for those Presidents who truly strove to do what they believed to be best for our nation above what was best for their party or themselves.

Day 307

I am thankful to have the right to vote for those who will be responsible for the direction and leadership of my community, my state, and my nation. I am grateful for every citizen who exercises that right, whether or not they vote for the same candidates or issues. I am grateful for those who have taken seriously the responsibilities of their elected positions and genuinely tried to better their communities. I am grateful for the systems of checks and balances in our government that have worked for two centuries. I believe that these systems would still work if not abused and exploited for the benefit of a few members of society who are either unwilling to work, or at least, unwilling to work within the system.

Day 308

I am grateful for multiple outlet power strips. These cords help distribute the available power over more devices. Only one wall outlet is being used, yet so many things can work from it. I am thankful for the people in my life who have encouraged me while encouraging others. Ultimately, there is still only one power source, yet so many people can glean from it. I am thankful for those whom the Lord has used me to encourage. It is satisfying and fulfilling to know you have been instrumental in either lightening the burden or brightening the day of a fellow traveler.

Day 309

I am grateful for extension cords. Depending on the length and dexterity of the cord, the power provided can travel almost anywhere. We can seek to be connected to the true source of power and then carry it wherever we are willing to go. We should be extensions of all the power and riches we have discovered wherever we may be. Are we kind at the grocery store? In traffic? Are we patient at church? At home? Are we actively extending the grace we have been given in our everyday lives? I am grateful for those who have extended to me the power found in kindness, patience, and forgiveness.

Day 310

Today, I would like to express my thankfulness for the cleaning supplies that help us keep our homes clean in a quick and efficient manner. I am talking about spray on bubbles that practically clean the shower for us, disinfectant wipes, and other useful sprays and deodorizers. Also, I am thankful that God makes it just as simple for us to keep ourselves clean before Him: "If we confess our sins, He is faithful and just to forgive us our sins." It is only pride, then, that causes us to keep our wrongs in our heart; the unwillingness to confess when we are guilty. I am thankful that Jesus always wants us to come to Him and that He always is ready and willing to forgive.

Day 311

Vanilla or caramel, sea breeze or fresh linen, pumpkin spice or mixed berries: I enjoy a room permeated with the scent of a candle. There are so many scents from which to choose now. I appreciate when others put that little extra effort into welcoming their guests by lighting candles. I have some friends like this, too. They just add that little "extra" to the occasion just because they are there. They listen a little longer; they ask a few more questions; they make others feel that they genuinely care. I have a friend who likes to mix the scents of different candles and make her house smell "extra pretty." I like to think that is how my friends are mixed. I am thankful for candles and friends that lend that little "extra" to the occasions of life.

Day 312

Recently here in Monterrey we sang (in Spanish of course) "I Have Decided to Follow Jesus." I recognized the tune and I could read the words. As I sang it, I remembered a time a group of us teenagers were challenged to mean the words we were singing. I took that challenge which eventually led me here. I am thankful that the steps of Jesus are not difficult to trace. I am grateful that someone cared enough about a group of teenagers to issue the challenge to us. I am thankful that I decided to follow. I am thankful for all of the steps of my journey and for each path that I have crossed. I am grateful that when Jesus calls us to follow He then walks each step with us.

Day 313

Composing a few entries about some of my favorite Bible stories caused me to remember the "Who Am I?" cards. My Mom played these with my brother and me often when we were very young. I remember her using them to teach us about the blessings of obedience and honesty, and the punishments of disobedience and dishonesty. I believe this foundation helped us to develop a better understanding of sin and to be more receptive to Christ's payment of our penalty for it.* I am thankful for children's games of Bible knowledge and adults who take the time to enjoy them with the children.

please see epilogue for more information regarding this decision

Day 314

Do you remember how exciting it was to find the prize in the box of cereal? Or how comforting it felt to wake up to Mom making oatmeal or cream of wheat? Do you remember your favorite cereal as a kid? Mine was Cap'n Crunch only to be topped by Peanut Butter Cap'n Crunch when that came out *(yes, I am that old)*. To this day I love to have cereal for breakfast or even sometimes in the evening when I am watching TV. I know that boxed cereal is only slightly nutritious, but I am thankful for the comfort and the memories to be found in a bowl of Cheerios.

Day 315

I am thankful that I am able to look in the mirror and see myself as others see me. I can get that spaghetti sauce off of my chin, or the broccoli from between my teeth. I can curl or smooth my hair or look for small imperfections that may distract others from my words or my teaching. I am thankful, too, for the times I have seen myself reflected in the actions of others. The nature of my job for many years has involved large quantities of time spent with small children. Sometimes I can see my own pettiness or selfishness reflected in their behavior regarding blocks, or dolls, or trucks. Is it really that important for me to have my own way that I had to "push out" someone else? Would it hurt me to share more? The things that I sometimes think are so important are really nothing more than trifles. I am thankful for mirrors, and I am thankful for reflections in others that help me see myself more clearly.

Day 316

I am thankful for the story of Esther, the peasant girl who becomes the queen. Scripture does not reveal much to us about her life before she was summoned to the palace: How old was she when her parents died? Did she have a job? Did she already have a suitor? Did she even want to be the queen? We may never know those answers, but we do know that when she had the opportunity to save her people – her friends, her family, her neighbors, her nation – that she rose to the challenge. Perhaps those other details were left out of the story because they do not matter. Esther was a young woman who perceived what the will of God was for her "at such a time as this" and let nothing stand between her and the accomplishment of His will. I am thankful that each of us, in no matter what circumstances we presently find ourselves, can perceive what the will of God is for this time of our lives and accomplish it. Past failures nor past victories really matter in what we are to accomplish today.

Day 317

I am thankful for the opportunity I am being given here in Mexico to teach and influence the lives of young people whose parents were led to the Lord by a man and his wife who have been faithful missionaries for over forty years. And, though the pastor and administrators may have considered my previous experience, the students in the classroom only desire to know what I am going to do now. It does not matter to them how many students only passed algebra because I tutored them, or how many years I taught first grade. What is important now is how much I care about them and how much of myself I am willing to give in order for them to become better students, better citizens, better Christians, and better people. I clearly see God's will for me right now. I am thankful that each of us who will diligently seek Him, can know exactly what is right for us to do this day.

Day 318

I am thankful for the stories in the life of Daniel. Here is a young man who did well in his studies and tried to honor his parents only to be taken as a servant and made to finish his studies in Babylon. I have often wondered why all the other young men did not also refuse the king's meat. I am thankful that Daniel purposed to do right and to honor his God. I am thankful for his three friends who refused to bow to the statue of the king. I am thankful for Christians who purpose to take the Gospel to lands where they may be persecuted. I am thankful that if in our lifetimes we are called upon to stand for right we can have the same confidence and determination because we know that the story will always end in victory; even if that victory is not seen here on earth.

Day 319

I am thankful for faithful men and women of God who have left their footprints for our generation. I am thankful that in a world run rampant with adultery and fornication committed even by those who are, or are at least claim to be Christians, there are still husbands and wives who are faithful to each other. I am thankful there are still young people who are willing to wait for marriage. I am grateful that in a world being run more and more by the fear of upsetting children, that there are still parents who properly discipline their children. I am thankful that in the wake of common core and new math that there are still teachers who regard the education of their students above political buzz words. I am grateful for these every day "Daniels" who choose the high road over the easy way. I am thankful for the ordinary heroes who make our world better every day.

Day 320

"Tell me the stories of Jesus, write on my heart every word." I am thankful for the stories in the Gospels that show us the humanity of Jesus while telling us of His wondrous miracles. I am thankful to know that Jesus got tired sometimes; that He felt hungry sometimes; and that on at least one occasion He was overcome with anger. I am also grateful for the stories that tell us of His ability to command the oceans and the tides, as well as the storms and the skies. I am glad to know, to absolutely KNOW that God can calm whatever storm may find me today; He can calm whatever unpleasant circumstance I may create for myself today for lack of paying attention to what is happening around me. Sometimes, though, He chooses to hold my hand, or to hold me close, and let the storm rage on. I am thankful that I can rest in the knowledge that God is in complete control of everything that is happening in my world.

Day 321

I am thankful, too, for the stories of the disciples. At different times, I have identified with different ones of the twelve. I have often been like Peter, the out-spoken know-it-all. In more than one situation my friends have accused me of having standards higher than God's, which ranks me with the Pharisaical Matthew, expecting more from others than God does, and coming across judgmentally. Along with James and John who desired to sit next to Jesus' throne, I have felt more strongly the desire to be recognized for my accomplishments or even my efforts than my desire to give all the glory to God. I am thankful that God chose to show us the shortcomings of the disciples and the way in which He lovingly rebuked them and taught them the proper responses. I hope that I have matured in some of these areas; but it is good to be reminded sometimes of just how patient Jesus has been with us.

Day 322

Blue has always been my favorite color. I chose blue in all the games when I was a kid. I wore blue as often as I possibly could. I remember one Easter being terribly upset with my mother because she "made" me wear a yellow dress. I enjoy looking up at the blue sky and I enjoy looking out across the blue waters of lakes or oceans. I am thankful that our world consists of many, many colors. I am especially thankful for blue, my favorite color.

Day 323

Sore throat season is upon us. Invariably I will have a cough and / or a sore throat most of the winter. I am thankful for the soothing power of tea and honey as well as the sterilizing power of hydrogen peroxide. I remember thinking of it as an unfair punishment when Dad made me gargle with it as a kid. After all, I did not give myself a sore throat on purpose. But, I am so thankful that it works. To be sure, the honey tastes better and feels better going down; but it only soothes, it does not heal. The awful, yucky hydrogen peroxide is what killed the bacteria and germs that caused the illness. There really are two sides to every coin. In dealing with children for most of my life I have learned that every personality trait has both positives and negatives. We can develop the positive sides of our personalities into good character traits; and whittle down the negative traits into mere minor annoyances. It may not have tasted good going down, but I am thankful for those "hydrogen peroxide" learning times that have helped develop my character.

Day 324

Anyone who knows me at all would be shocked if I made it through the winter without mentioning how much I enjoy the warmth and prevention provided by scarves. I wear one almost every day of the season. I am thankful for colorful scarves and plain, ordinary scarves. I am especially thankful for my "teacher scarf" hand made one year by one of my students for a birthday present. It is yellow with black on one end which comes to a point. The other end has a band of gray just before it is rounded off in pink to look like an eraser. I love to wear it and almost always get comments about my pencil scarf. I am thankful for the opportunities I have been given to prevent complications and heartaches from coming into my life. I am grateful that some of them have been fun and exciting (I enjoyed attending a Christian college). Some of them were plain and ordinary (developing and maintaining good habits). Some of them were bold and colorful; but they all served the same purpose. Regardless of how they felt or appeared, I am thankful to have been spared the trouble, guilt, or pain that could have been caused by a reckless or rebellious youth.

Day 325

I am thankful for window blinds. With a twist of the pole I can let in the sunshine or filter it to exactly as much as I can stand. I can pull the cord and see out the window the same as if the blinds were not even there. At nighttime, I can peek out and see whose dog that is or if everyone else's lights also went out when I heard that thunder. I am also thankful that God has given me a similar "filter" for my heart. I do not have to "wear my feelings on my sleeve." But, when it is time, and when the right friend is yielding a sympathetic ear, I can filter as much as I want to share, then pull the cord and go on with the rest of the day. I can share with the young people whom I am teaching the times I experienced similar disappointments or discouragements. I can let them see that I am real and that I need help sometimes just like they do. Yes, I am grateful for window blinds and I am also grateful for heart blinds.

Day 326 Thanksgiving

All across the country today, Sunday School Teachers, Pastors, and Youth Pastors will be admonishing those in their charge to think about people and things for which they should be grateful. If you have been following these writings this year, hopefully, you will be able to comprise a thoughtful and inclusive list. I am grateful that on this Sunday, one year ago, my Pastor did just that and thus began this 365-day journal. I encourage you to not be satisfied only with reading mine, but to start your own journey.

Day 327 Thanksgiving

I am thankful for my childhood memories surrounded by the traditions of Thanksgiving. My Gramma would make a large turkey and a small ham. No one has ever been able to match my Mom's dressing. My aunts would make mashed potatoes, green beans, and orange jello salad. There would be broccoli and cauliflower covered in cheese; and sweet potatoes covered in marshmallows. And so many people! -- aunts, uncles, cousins, friends from out-of-town. It was always a good time with lots of good food and plenty of leftovers.

Day 328 Thanksgiving

There will always be a special place in my heart for those families who remember those without, or unable to be with, families on special holidays such as Thanksgiving. Growing up, our family was one such family. We often included the single teachers from our Christian school (not just at Thanksgiving). Many times that I have been unable to visit my family I have been the recipient of the generosity of others. I believe I was reaping what my parents had sown. It is always nice to be included and many of these families treated me like family, if even only for the day.

Day 329 Thanksgiving

I am thankful for special Wednesday night church services on the eve of Thanksgiving: when as a church family we can rehearse the blessings of the soon-ending year; when we can rejoice in the blessings of our fellow-parishoners. My home church in Arkansas celebrates with "Prayer, Praise, & Pie!" I am thankful for the opportunity for us to express our gratitude publicly.

Day 330 Thanksgiving Day

Of course, today, I am thankful for Thanksgiving. I am grateful for the pilgrims and separatists who set sail for "The New World." I am grateful for the pioneers who braved untold hardships to forge our great nation. I am thankful that President Lincoln proclaimed that Americans should set aside this day each year for the sole purpose of demonstrating gratitude for the bountiful blessings and tremendous heritage that we have been given.

Day 331

While some people today may be thankful for shopping, I am thankful for an extra day of rest and relaxation. I am thankful that I have only been shopping once in my life on the Friday after Thanksgiving. I am thankful that for many of us the Christmas season has officially begun. We will pull out the Christmas music as we enjoy our leftover Turkey sandwiches. When I am able to travel to visit with them, I am thankful for an extra day to spend with my family.

Day 332

Maybe today you are still enjoying leftovers from your bountiful meal. Maybe today you are squeezing in one more day relaxing with family you do not get to see often enough. Maybe today you will start your Christmas shopping. Whatever the case, today I am thankful for this extra little day, Saturday, tucked in just enough before Christmas to still be considered part of Thanksgiving. However it may be spent, let us all be thankful for it. And may we be reminded to be thankful for all of the "extras" we enjoy. Every day, we receive more than we deserve. Every day we are given little bonuses that we often fail to realize are even there. This year, I noticed more of them because I decided to write about them. But what I learned is the more I looked for the extras, the more I found. So on this extra day, I will be determined to be more grateful for more of life's little extras.

Day 333

In several Sunday entries I have listed different things about different Pastors in my life for whom I am grateful. Today, though, I would like to share a thought or two about their wives. Every Pastor's Wife daily sacrifices her "normal" in hopes that our lives might maintain their normalcy in the midst of crisis or chaos. Or, as the wife of one of my former Pastors said often: "Around here, normal is just a setting on the dryer." Their husbands are often at the hospital in the middle of the night, ministering at the prison, preaching in the nursing home, or comforting the family at the funeral home. Your Pastor's Wife sends meals to the sick or bereaved; loves and prays for your home and your children; heads up the dinner on the grounds and the Women's Missionary Societies. I am grateful for the example of selflessness that I have seen through the life of each Pastor's Wife with whom I have served.

Day 334

As November comes to a close and our minds begin to turn toward snow and winter and Christmas, I am thankful for this month of gratitude. Many of us are more verbal with our thankfulness in this, the month of Thanksgiving. Many of us spend more time counting our blessings. Many of us genuinely are more grateful. I am thankful for those who serve from a heart full of Thanksgiving. I am thankful for each person who remembers that everything we have truly is a gift. I am thankful for this season of thankfulness.

December

Day 335

I am grateful for the old holiday classic stand-by's of "Frosty" and "Rudolph." Growing up, we were always sure to know what night and channel they were going to come on, and all the kids watched them. My favorite is "Frosty." I got a DVD of this when one of my friend's little boy was two years old and watched it over and over with him with cookies and hot chocolate! It became our Christmas tradition. We watched it every year for twelve years; we may still have observed this tradition had I not moved away. "Frosty" and "Rudolph" helped us enjoy Christmas while teaching us a little lesson about ourselves. I am thankful that God made me who I am; that He placed me where I am, surrounded by those who love me, regardless of whether or not they understand me; and, that He gave me the job He made me to do. I am thankful that "Frosty" does return and I am thankful that the misfit toys all found a home. And, I am thankful that I have, too.

Day 336

I am also thankful for the adult Christmas classic movies. My two personal favorites are "Miracle on 34th Street" and "It's a Wonderful Life." I can quote some of the lines from these two, but more importantly, we can learn to live some of the lines. I wonder if we really do think the intangibles are more important than the tangibles? Do we truly value and appreciate our friends? I am thankful that I can still believe in the magic and the spirit of Christmas! I am thankful for the intangibles I have accumulated which can be shared, but never taken away.

Day 337

I am thankful for books that are classics at Christmas-time. The Velveteen Rabbit by Margery Williams is definitely one of my all-time favorites! I took some of the passages from this children's book as my personal definitions for the words "love" and "real." One of my favorites to read out loud is How the Grinch Stole Christmas, by Dr. Seuss. Of course, I watched it, too, when it was made into a cartoon. I am grateful for these wonderful stories that help convey to children that "Christmas" lives in us. It cannot be stolen or even squelched. Christmas is so much more than toys and trees and sweets. Christmas is the celebration of the greatest Gift ever given!

Day 338

I am thankful for Charles Schulz' Peanuts' Holiday Classics. How could any of us ever forget Charlie Brown's Christmas tree or Linus' recitation of the Christmas story? This was another one of those, though now available on DVD, that was once highly anticipated for its annual appearance. I am thankful that in these children's classics, the true meaning of Christmas is not lost. Though not all of them explicitly share the original Christmas story as well as this one, the meaning of Christmas was not obscured by the getting of gifts or the manipulation of family members. I am thankful for the beginning of the Christmas season!

Day 339

To be sure, Christmas is a family holiday, filled with special family traditions. But, today I am thankful for those families who included me as part of their Christmas celebrations when I was unable to share this special holiday with my own family. I am thankful for those who opened their homes and allowed me to be a part of the family for a short while. I am thankful for the gifts, the food, and the fun. Most of all, though, I am thankful for the love that prompted the invitation.

Day 340

I am thankful for Christmas Carols! I love to rejoice in and sing about the birth of the Saviour. I enjoy playing them on CD or through Pandora. I enjoy singing them in the car and around the house. But, I am especially thankful to hear them at church. I am grateful for the choir members who have been practicing since October for the Cantata or other special programs. I am thankful for the song leaders who choose these hymns for the season. I am truly thankful for Christmas carols.

Day 341

I am also thankful for Christmas caroling and Christmas carolers. The tradition has died out somewhat in the technological age, but it is still welcomed and encouraged in most places. My home church in Arkansas would plan the evening around nearby neighborhoods, some church members who could not get out and about, then end walking through downtown Hot Springs singing loudly and proudly. I am thankful for those who still remember the reason for the season.

Day 342

I am also thankful that there are other ways of acknowledging the reason for the season. I can remember when everyone spelled out C-H-R-I-S-T-M-A-S. I am thankful for those who still do. Using an "X" seems to "mark out" Christ to me. Probably everyone who uses that abbreviation does not have that intent, but it still has the same feel regardless of the intent. I am grateful for those who purposely keep "Christ" in "Christmas."

Day 343 Christmas Memories

My parents always let us choose one gift to open on Christmas Eve. My Dad would read the Christmas story from Luke 2 while we drank hot chocolate and ate Christmas cookies. The anticipation and excitement would mount while we sat by the Christmas tree and perused the wrapped boxes one last time. When we were small, we almost always chose the largest box for our first gift; as we grew older, we became a little more selective. I am grateful that my parents made special family time for "just us" a part of our Christmas memories. I am grateful that my parents were able to purchase presents for us and that the receiving of these presents was always preceded by taking time to remember the greatest Gift ever given to any of us. I am truly thankful for so many good memories associated with my family Christmases.

Day 344 Christmas Memories

Then, on Christmas morning, we would awaken to the other gifts under the tree along with a few more from Santa. I remember one year, one of those gifts was a big blue teddy bear that I had named Snuggles while he was still in the store. I was certain that it was the same bear, not a new one from the North Pole. We always found little things in our stockings that my Mom knew we would enjoy; usually new crayons and toothbrushes, some chocolate, and almost always something special for each of us that the other did not get. I am thankful for Christmas morning. I am grateful for the excitement and anticipation that it brings; but, even more importantly, I am grateful for the love that it envelops.

Day 345 Christmas Memories

One Christmas when we were a little older and beginning to debate whether or not there really was a Santa Claus, my parents allowed us to stay up on Christmas Eve and watch for him. Of course, after a while we fell asleep. But, around one or two in the morning we were jolted awake by the sound of jingling bells and hoofbeats on the roof. My Mom ran outside with us to see if we could see him, or at least a glimpse of his sleigh. We even heard a deep bass "Ho, ho, ho!" and I thought I heard his whip (my brother said Santa did not need a whip for his reindeer). When we were convinced that he was gone, we went back in the house to tell my Dad all about it. He must have been really, really, tired because he slept through all of that commotion! I am thankful for so many things about Christmas and the Christmas season. I am thankful that I really got to enjoy Christmas as a child.

Day 346 Christmas Memories

On Christmas Day, we usually had dinner at my Gramma's house with aunts, uncles, cousins, and usually some friends whose families lived out of town. It was crowded and loud, happy and boisterous. There was always a "kid's table." There was sooo much food! Turkey, ham, and all the things you can imagine to go with them. Cookies, candies, and pies were all home-made. My mom and her sister, with the "help" of their kids, would spend weeks before Christmas making literally tons of cookies, fudge, divinity, and chocolates. A box with a variety of these sweets was their gift to friends, neighbors, bosses, pastors, almost everyone they loved. And, of course, there was plenty of it at Gramma's – one whole table had nothing on it but an assortment of fudge! I am thankful for these memories and for the spirit of giving that permeated the atmosphere. I am thankful for the bountiful blessings that I enjoyed as a child without even realizing how blessed I truly was.

Day 347 The Christmas Story

"And it came to pass in those days that there went out a decree from Caesar Augustus that all the world should be taxed …" No doubt many Sunday School classes and children's choirs have already begun memorizing this passage for a special Christmas presentation or play. No doubt many of you reading this entry also memorized portions of Luke 2 as a child. I am thankful for the Christmas story. The greatest story of love and hope that has ever been written is found in the Christmas story. I am thankful that Jesus chose to love me. I am thankful that Mary and Joseph chose to honor God even in what they could not comprehend of the Christmas story. "Glory to God in the highest, and on earth, peace, good will toward men."

Day 348 The Christmas Story

In Luke chapter one, we see the angel come to Mary to tell her she will carry in her womb the Son of God. He proclaims Jesus to be The King of Whose Kingdom there shall be no end. We see Mary, alone and afraid. We hear the Angel say "Fear not." We see Mary as a humble maiden engaged to a lowly carpenter. We hear the Angel tell her that she is blessed among women and that she has found favor with God. I am thankful for the words of the angel Gabriel used by God to show Mary who she truly was. Who we really are is rarely what others see us to be. I am thankful that God sees more in me than what appears to others. I am truly thankful that what God sees in me is more than what I can see.

Day 349 The Christmas Story

Not only am I thankful for the words spoken to Mary by Gabriel, I am also thankful for her response. We see first her fear and uncertainty; her humanity, if you will. But before the angel leaves, she speaks the words that we should choose as our daily prayer: "Behold the handmaid of the Lord; be it unto me according to Thy word." Mary knew she would have to face the man she loved and with whom she wanted to have a family with the news that she was with child. I am sure she hoped he would believe her incredulous story, but she had no guarantee. What would her parents or friends think of her? We have no record in Scripture of any but Joseph's reaction. But in the split-second that she was given to choose, she chose Christ. We are faced with decisions every day to choose to honor Christ. Will we take the high-road whether anyone else ever knows or not? What do we do when no one else is watching or ever likely to find out? I am thankful for Mary and for her decision to honor Christ.

Day 350 The Christmas Story

The angel also came to Joseph and gave Him a glimpse of this magnificent plan. The Bible tells us that while Joseph was thinking about how to handle this "problem" without embarrassing Mary, the angel comes to assure him that Mary is telling him the truth. Here is a man who truly loved his betrothed. He wanted to do what was best for her more than he wanted anything else. I am thankful also for his response found in verse 24: "Then Joseph … did as the angel of the Lord had bidden him …" I am thankful for Joseph and how God used him to bring about His marvelous plan. I am thankful that Joseph chose Mary. I am thankful that Joseph chose Jesus.

Day 351 The Christmas Story

I am grateful for the star that shone in the East to declare the coming of the King. I am thankful that every prophecy in the Old Testament regarding the birth of the Messiah was fulfilled exactly as it should have been. I am thankful for the "signs and wonders" that point all men to Him. But, I am also thankful for the seemingly common, ordinary things God uses to point men to Himself. The star we call the sun rises every morning and sets every evening. The waves rush to shore every second; then calmly recede again. Babies are born every day; and every day, someone slips into eternity. Miraculous surgeries are performed every day in every major city of the world. Every new day, I am given the gift of twenty-four non-refundable, non-returnable hours. Every day I can choose to love or hate; I can choose to forgive or to grow seeds of bitterness. Every day God allows me to choose to please Him or to please myself. I am grateful for the signs and wonders; but I am also grateful for the common and the ordinary.

Day 352 The Christmas Story

I am grateful for the ordinary manger in the ordinary stable that housed the extraordinary King of Kings. I am grateful that Christ chose to be born to a humble family of low degree. I am grateful that Christ chose to be born as an ordinary baby and to live an ordinary childhood. If He had chosen the palace and luxuries He so richly deserved, I am afraid many of us would never be able to relate to Him. We would be tempted to say that He is beyond our ability to comprehend. But Christ chose to live His extraordinary – above – all – other lives in such an ordinary, completely humble way. I am grateful that Christ chose to identify with ordinary people more than royalty. I am grateful for His example and His love; but most of all I am grateful for His mercy!

Day 353 The Christmas Story

When I was in second grade I remember that we did a little play about the animals in the manger on the first Christmas. Each of us had a line to say representing what each animal would say if the animals could talk. I am not sure why I remember it, but my part was the donkey and my line (that rhymed of course; and which my mother declared was the best animal in the program) was something to the effect of even though he was oh, so tired, how glad he was that he was chosen to carry Mary and her baby to the stable. Other animals represented by my classmates were a cow, a horse, others I do not remember, and, of course, the sheep. I hope that I am always glad, even though I may grow oh, so weary, to be chosen to carry Christ to others. I am thankful for children's Christmas plays: and I am thankful for opportunities to carry Christ to others.

Day 354 Christmas Memories

The official beginning of winter is sometime today. When I was a small child, it seemed that winter nor Christmas would ever come. When I lived in the North it seemed that winter began sometime in October. Likewise, when I was young, I thought that my winter, my old age, would never come. I thought I would be young forever. And, though while for me it is still fall, it seems that winter is looming nearer. Next year at this time I will celebrate a milestone birthday that some consider to be the brink of our older years. I am thankful that all that winter brings is not undesirable. I am thankful that in my winter I can be excited still for snowflakes and snowfalls. I can look forward still to birthdays and Christmases. I hope that as I enjoyed my summer, so I might also enjoy my winter. I hope to be able to be grateful in the end for a life well-lived.

Day 355 Christmas Memories

My Mom always made a big deal of my birthday. My presents were never wrapped in Christmas paper. I always got to pick the cake I wanted, and my Mom always made it for me; even my birthdays that she was battling cancer. My Mom always sent birthday cookies to school the week before Christmas break and asked the teacher if she could do it on a different day than the class Christmas party. Today, I am thankful for all of the special memories that surround my birthday.

Day 356 Christmas Memories

The only time that I remember my Mom not being well enough to celebrate and bake for my birthday, my Dad took me out for a special date. He treated me out to an early breakfast; we went to the mall and looked at typewriters (note: Laptops had not yet been invented). We looked at five or six different types of typewriters. We finally decided on the new-fangled kind that wrote with a ball-point pen. I used that typewriter all through college and through my beginning teaching years. My dad had overheard me say to one of my friends how much I would like to have one for my college papers. I had not asked for one because I knew my family was struggling with my college tuition, my brother's high school tuition, and the twenty percent of uncovered medical expenses for my Mom's treatments. Somehow, though, my dad managed to find the money for something that I especially wanted. He never told me, but looking back, I am sure he sold something or took on an extra project to be able to afford to make my birthday extra special. I am thankful for all of the wonderful memories of the Christmas holidays especially those that include my birthday.

Day 357 The Christmas Story

I am grateful for the shepherds in the story of Christmas. Here were faithful men, doing their job on the hillside where they must have been many other nights before. But this night would be different. This night would mark a milestone in the history of the world. After this night, nothing would ever be the same again! I am thankful that God chose shepherds, the lowest of all vocations, to be the first to hear of the birth of His Son. I am thankful that they went "with haste" to the place where the Baby lay. I am thankful that their excitement and enthusiasm is still shared by children of all ages during the Christmas season!

Day 358 The Christmas Story

The wise men are almost always included in the nativity scenes displayed throughout the world during Christmas. I know the Bible tells of their coming much later, after Mary and Joseph had already settled into a house and were no longer in the stable. But I am grateful that their story is included in the traditional Christmas renditions. It took them a lot longer to arrive at the place where Jesus was than the shepherds. They encountered obstacles not encountered by the shepherds. They had to be more determined to find the Christ-child even after the excitement and enthusiasm had waned. I am grateful for the wise men and for their gifts. I am grateful that the Christ-child accepts all who come to Him, and that it can never be too late.

Day 359 Christmas Day

I am thankful that Christ chose to leave Heaven and come to earth as a baby, so that He could grow into a man Who would die for my sin. There are so many songs and plays that direct our attention to this fact during this season, but one of my favorites is a children's program which asks us to imagine the hustle and bustle in the Heavens as the angels prepared to usher the Messiah to Bethlehem. One of the songs features different angels discussing how they think he should cross the threshold into earth. One thinks He should be a general, commanding a mighty army; another thinks He should be a wealthy singer; another, a king; and so on. Of course, when they are told He will go as not just a baby, but a poor baby, born to ordinary parents, the angels are aghast with disbelief. None of this is in the Bible, I know; but have you ever stopped and thought about just what it meant for the King of Glory, the Creator of the Universe, the All-powerful, to relinquish all of Heaven to reclaim you for Himself. I am thankful that "God so loved the world that He gave." I am thankful that He loved me that much, and all I have to do is to accept His Christmas gift of eternal life.

please see epilogue for more information regarding this decision

Day 360

Not much recognized in the United States, but a regular Canadian tradition is observed on this day every year – Boxing Day. To express gratitude for the many blessings received during the previous year and especially over the holidays, many people will "box" some of their abundance of items: food, clothing, toys, heaters, . . . anything; and give them to those less fortunate. Although, I have not done this in observance of this particular day, I have been fortunate enough to donate to shelters, and organizations such as The Salvation Army and The Goodwill. I am grateful that I do have an abundance of material things. Even considering all of the "worldly goods" with which I parted before moving to Mexico, I still have an over-abundance compared to most of the people who live here. I am grateful that I have enough to share. I am grateful for those who share with me. I am also grateful that we can never out-give the Lord.

Day 361

On the Sunday between Christmas and the New Year no doubt many of us will resolve to read our Bible every day in the new year; maybe we will even resolve to read it all the way through. I am thankful that I was challenged to do this as a very young person. I am grateful that my parents encouraged me to read the Bible. I am thankful for Bible-reading schedules and Pastors who encourage their people to use them. I am most thankful for the guidance and direction I have received by doing so.

Day 362

No doubt, there will also be many other resolutions decided upon this week: resolutions to eat better, exercise more, read more, spend more time with the children, and many other worthwhile endeavors. I am grateful that someone taught me to set specific goals: "I am going to eat at least one fruit and one vegetable each day. I am going to exercise thirty minutes each day. I am going to read one book per month. I am going to spend Tuesday night doing something I can enjoy with my children." I am thankful that I still have goals to set, that there are still things I want to accomplish with whatever time may be left in my life. I want to do at least one thing every day that will out-live me. It may be as simple as saying one kind word to the person who needs it most, or it may be as profound as finishing a chapter of my next book. I am not sure but that the kind word may last longer.

Day 363

Today I am grateful for each of you who have taken the time to read my humble thoughts on gratitude. I trust that if you have read this long, you will finish with me. I am thankful for how much I have learned and grown simply by taking a little time each day to be thankful for something in my life. It has been my sincere desire that we have grown together on this journey of thankfulness. I am grateful for every person reading this who desires to become a more grateful person.

Day 364

I have spent the past year intentionally thinking of something for which to be grateful every day. Some days it was very easy, some days, not so much. After tomorrow, I will stop writing these entries, but I truly hope I will not stop looking for ways to express my gratitude. I sincerely desire to seek for the good and the positive even when it may seem that there is none. I am thankful that when I was still in high school I was encouraged to choose a life's verse. The teacher who prompted us to do so said it should be a verse that we could claim throughout our lives as a special message from God to us and that we should not hurry or choose it lightly. So today, I am thankful for the verses I chose at age seventeen: the year my Mom was diagnosed with cancer, the year my Dad's job required a sixty-minute one-way commute, the year I started college, the year the church in which I had grown up dissolved, the year everything that I had known changed completely. The year I learned that God is the only true constant in our lives. Through these verses I learned that no matter how bleak are our circumstances, we can be so grateful that God is always there and always in control and that we will triumph before the end of the story.

"Although the fig tree shall not blossom, neither shall fruit be in the vines; the labour of the olive shall fail, and the fields shall yield no meat; the flock shall be cut off from the fold, and there shall be no herd in the stalls: Yet I will rejoice in the Lord, I will joy in the God of my salvation. The Lord God is my strength, and He will make my feet like hinds' feet, and He will make me to walk upon mine high places ..."

Day 365

Today, this year is ending, as will someday all of our years. Allow me to say without sounding pious or holier-than-thou that I am thankful to still be serving the Lord, to still know what His purposes are concerning me, and to be content in His will. I am thankful to be able to say that the sentiments of the following selection to the best of my knowledge are still true. If you will, another poem from my youth, written at age eighteen, "My February":

Well, it's winter now and all the leaves are gone

It's kinda funny how

Time flies by so quickly!

Someday I will be in the February of me.

My own personal wintertime

When all the leaves are bare

And I'm sure I will discover a little gray within my hair

I just hope, that then, as now,

In the springtime of my life

I will know what I am doing and why I am doing it

Also, just because there will be a little slush upon the ground

Doesn't mean I'll have to slush around

And just because there are no leaves in the trees

Doesn't mean the birds won't sing

And if they can sing with icicles at their feet

Surely, I, with Jesus at my side

Can sing a joyous melody

When I trudge through

My February

Epilogue

The Most Important Decision

I would like to personally thank you for taking the time to read my humble thoughts regarding gratitude. If however you have never received **the** most important of all gifts, the only one that can assure us of an eternal Home with the Lord in Heaven, please continue reading the Scripture selections included below:

1. We do not deserve Heaven: *"For all have sinned and come short of the glory of God."* – *Romans 3:23.* At one time or another we have all chosen to disobey God.
2. Our sin has a penalty: *"For the wages {payment} of sin is death; but the gift of God is eternal life through Jesus Christ our Lord." – Romans 6:23.* The payment for our disobedience is Spiritual death and Hell. (Matthew 25:46, Revelation 21:8)
3. Jesus paid our penalty: *"But God commendeth {proved} his love toward us, in that, while we were yet sinners, Christ died for us." – Romans 5:8.* God proved His love for us by giving His only Son to die on the cross for our sin. Jesus rose again the third day *{Easter}*, conquering death and Hell, and paying our penalty for sin.
4. We must believe on Jesus and accept His payment for our sin: *"That if thou shalt confess with thy mouth the Lord Jesus, and shalt believe in thine heart that God hath raised Him from the dead, thou shalt be saved." – Romans 10:9.* To believe on Jesus Christ as Saviour means to have faith that He died for you, paid the price for your sin, and is **the only** way to Heaven. You can express your belief on Jesus through prayer, but it is the faith and belief that assures you of His acceptance. There are no "magic words."
5. Pray sincerely after this example: "Dear Jesus, I know that I am a sinner and do not deserve Heaven. I believe that You died on the cross, paid the penalty for my sin, and rose again after three days. I am placing my faith and trust in You alone to forgive my sin and take me to Heaven when I die. Thank you for Your gift of eternal life! In Jesus' name, Amen."

Again, thank you for taking the time to read my thoughts. If you have made any decisions as a result of this writing I would sincerely love to know about them. If you have any specific questions or concerns with which I could help you, or prayer requests to share, I would certainly appreciate the opportunity to be a blessing. I can best be contacted by e-mail through my company, superiorscholasticskills@gmail.com.

Made in the USA
Columbia, SC
27 March 2019